DITCHES TO
RICHES

J	JALAPENO
M	MEAT
S	STICK
P	PUBLISHING

Jalapeño Meat Stick Publishing
1009 9th Street
Greeley, CO 80631
(970) 396-0589

ISBN: 978-1-7355160-0-4 (print)

ISBN: 978-1-7355160-1-1 (ebook)

ISBN: 978-1-7355160-2-8 (audiobook)

Ordering Information:
Special discounts are available on quantity purchases by corporations, associations, and others. For details, contact Ron@ronworley.com

CONTENTS

DITCHES TO RICHES

HOW TO SURVIVE YOUR F&%$ED-UP LIFE AND CREATE A KICK-ASS BUSINESS

RONALD L WORLEY II

CHAPTER 1:
FROM DITCHES

"Are you okay?"

That jogger's question woke me up and probably saved my life.

The truck I was driving had rolled three times, throwing me from the vehicle. I was five miles from the smallest town in Nebraska, face down in a ditch.

Miraculously, at least to me, that jogger just happened to be running near the site of my accident. Had he not been there, who knows what would have happened.

As I lay there face down, I tried to lift my head, but it was so heavy I could only raise it off the dirt…just high enough to see two white socks and a pair of well-used running shoes. My head ached and blood ran into my eyes, making it hard to see.

Just before passing out, a question ran through my head, "What the hell have I done?"

Hours passed before I awoke in a hospital bed surrounded by many faces—none of which were familiar to me.

The face that stuck out was that of a grumpy old cop. His tan skin reminded me of an elephant's butt. This cop immediately demanded information about the accident. I had been conscious less than a minute before the interrogation began. My memory slowly returned as he questioned me.

He tried to get me to confess to being the driver of the pickup they found upside down on a rural country road. I'd had enough encounters with the law to know it would not be in my best interest to admit to anything…especially to being the driver of that truck. The last thing I needed was a fourth DUI. He demanded my ID, which I didn't have. It was taken a week earlier when I was arrested for my third DUI.

As he continued to question me, my head would not stop spinning. I was a complete mess. Of course, I was still hung over from the night before, but I was also still quite buzzed from doing meth just a few hours earlier. Before the accident, I was on my way to town to get more beer. As is common practice with many addicts, I was able to lie on the spot without thought.

"I wasn't driving. Someone else was driving. I'm new to town; I can't remember his name. Wait! He's friends with the guy I'm living with…Jason." As soon as I mentioned my roommate, my mental fog cleared enough to realize Jason—and his wife—were standing in the corner, just past the officer who was interrogating me. "Damn it!" I thought to myself.

Jason looked at me quizzically and said, "Who are you talking about?" Jason knew I was lying.

I was an addict and most everything I said was a lie and Jason knew that answer was too. He kept his mouth shut for me but later called me out for it. Jason was a good man, worked hard, and had values that he used daily. I was big trouble for him, but Jason and his wife were not angels. We had done drugs together in the past, and they did smoke weed daily but they were very functional at the time. I was not.

I began to describe a fictitious figure, knowing good and well that Jason would never be able to place a name with the description. As Jason and I volleyed back and forth about this mysterious man, the cop got more frustrated and threw a packet of paperwork on my bed and said, "Just fill this out," as he left the room.

After the cop left, the nurse began to describe my injuries. I had a severe road rash on the back of my scalp—as if someone had run a cheese grater over it several times. All the ligaments in my right knee had been torn. There were various spots of road rash covering my body and my neck hurt terribly. They had done a full body x-ray while I was unconscious and, miraculously, I didn't have any broken bones.

As I sobered up in that hospital bed, my mind cleared, and I began to remember the events that led up to my accident. I remembered the early morning drive to the liquor store after Jason let me know that he and his wife were leaving for the day. In my head, I thought about how drunk I was going to get with the house to myself.

Jason had the most beautiful house I had ever seen at that point in my life. It had endless square feet and a basement with a game room, pool table, and a theater room, all set on 50 acres in the middle of nowhere Nebraska. I could not wait to be alone in that house.

Jason's friend, Mike, had borrowed my Pontiac Sunfire because his truck had an extreme amount of horsepower and a very loose front end. It was very dangerous on dirt roads, thus the reason Mike needed my car. So I concocted a plan to get into town to buy more liquor (I was not supposed to use Mike's truck). As soon as Jason and his wife left, I jumped in the truck and headed to town. Mike's truck was a thing of beauty, a grey S10, 450-hp, rear-wheel drive with a blower that stuck out of the hood. It was a beast and required some skill to drive. He warned me not to drive it. But I was hung over and wanted beer.

"Town is only five miles away, and I'll be back before anyone notices," I thought to myself.

Man, that truck was nice! When I turned the key in the ignition and the engine fired, it sounded like a car at the racetrack. I could feel the power of the motor in the seat as I slammed the gas pedal a couple of times just for fun. I imagined that I was a badass and could drive this bitch hard! I tested the truck as I crept out the long driveway that led out Jason's property.

I remember the steering wheel was super tight like a racecar's. And the rear end just wanted to go but it was too light to carry the horsepower of the motor. Once on the dirt road, I stayed in first gear and was nursing it. I was maybe going 30 mph but I wanted to see what this baby could do.

I punched the gas, and the rear of the truck spun out sideways. I could not correct the steering fast enough and the right-side wheels dug in. The last thing I remember about the actual accident was my own foot kicking me in the forehead as I flew through the air.

Loser by Choice

Addicts will tell you feelings of shame are typical after a bender. I felt shame many times. I had another rollover accident just a year earlier. In that accident, I hit an intersection going 101 mph. When the car hit the cross street, it took air and jumped 30 feet before hitting the ground and squatting all four wheels. Without wheels, the car flew into the ditch where the front end dug in, causing it to flip six times end over end. My friend and I were tossed around in the car and then ejected out the back window. My friend was thrown first and sent through a barbed wire fence, nearly cutting his ear off. I was thrown later, hit by the rear of the car, and launched into a telephone pole. The car eventually stopped and landed on top of me, pushing me into the dirt a few inches. I had just enough room to breathe and pull my head out to yell for help. Thankfully, a farmer's kid heard the accident and was able to ram the car off me using his truck's bumper. So that was my first encounter face down in a ditch.

After finding myself face down in a ditch for the second time, I hit a new low. When you are that low, there's no place to go but up. My friends were disgusted with me. I was disgusted with myself! I felt hopeless and alone. During those first few days in the hospital, I wanted to stay sober, and I knew of only one person who could help me do that: My mom. She had achieved sobriety and had been riding my butt since I was 15 to stop drinking.

I knew calling my mom wouldn't be easy, as I had burned that bridge several times over with constant lies, deceit, and manipulation. But I broke down and called her from my hospital bed, asking her for help. "I don't care if you live or die in that hospital, I am done helping you!" she yelled and then hung up. The one person I could depend on, my mom, just essentially told me to "F*ck off!" What now?

The next day Jason's wife came to visit. I pleaded with her to get me out of the hospital...now! I couldn't wait for the doctor to release me. After much deliberation, she agreed and grabbed all my stuff and pulled the truck around to the front. I waited for the nurse to go into another patient's room, and I hoisted my broken and beaten body up from the hospital bed. I was still in my hospital gown, and my body was still riddled with pain, but I hopped down the hall, out the door, and into the "getaway vehicle."

The fear of having to face that crotchety old cop again, plus another DUI, was worth the pain I faced escaping from that hospital. I wasn't okay...and I realized I needed to make serious changes to my life or I wasn't going to live much longer.

I was a homeless addict, an alcoholic, and a drain on everyone I had contact with. I was dangerous to myself and others, plus I was estranged from my three kids who were living in another state. I had to change. I told Jason and his wife I was going to change. I promised myself I was going to change. But most of the time, change is easier said than done.

I spent the next three weeks in Jason's house nursing my injuries. He put me to work writing bids for his business. I was making money, but I used what I made to buy alcohol. To me, being drunk was an all-day event. I justified it by convincing myself it was all I could do to avoid the shakes. I drank all day, and I even drank at night when I couldn't sleep. I also stepped up my drug use. I'd regularly used drugs since childhood. My dad gave me marijuana when I was two years old—ostensibly to help me fall asleep. In my last week in Nebraska, Jason, his wife, and I spent three days using cocaine. So if I had been more truthful earlier, I would have written, I was a homeless addict: An alcoholic, a druggie, and a drain on everyone with whom I had contact. During those three days, I had used up my welcome by mooching off them and their drugs. I even stole a li'l cocaine rock out of their bag and hid it in the bathroom for me to do later. Jason caught me, and that pretty much ruined any trust they had left for me. Here I had been living with them rent-free, wrecked a car, couldn't work, and then I stole their drugs. Without any fanfare, I packed my car, stole $50 out of Jason's change jar (for gas), and headed to my brother's house in Greeley, Colorado.

Today, I couldn't steal a million dollars from a billionaire. I have amassed some wealth, of course, or I couldn't be writing a book like this with any expertise. My real riches are the family I hold dear and the friends I surround myself with. Today, I own three companies, and since leaving Nebraska, have bought, run, and sold five more. In the last 10 years, I have realized the importance of running businesses for my community, using values to drive that purpose. Questions I ask and answer each and every day are: Who did I save today? How many people did I help? Where can

I help next? I surround myself with people who can help me do that. Most of them I pay, but all of them are like-minded. My kids don't remember homeless dad, drug addict dad, or even think of me as business dad. I am just their dad. Toot! Toot! I turned around their lives, too, and I feel as though I've done a damn great job raising them. All three are going somewhere in their own lives. The favorite comment I hear about myself is, "He is real." That's how I try to be in all aspects, at business and at home. If there is only one takeaway from my past, it is that a fraud is a fraud, and I am not a fraud anymore. I will speak to you only about my own truths and experiences in business and in values.

Square One

I lived through a childhood riddled with beatings and drug abuse—complete warfare on my future adult self. I stopped the cycle for my children, and they don't even know what addiction looks like. In 2001, I took a bottle of sleeping pills. I overdosed in my car trying to drive to the hospital after realizing what I had just done. I ended up in someone's yard in my car. The police officers saved my ass by pulling me out of the car, starting CPR, and dumping charcoal into my gut. In 2003, I became homeless, thanks to the progression of my addictions and my selfishness. I lost my children for six months because I was homeless, hopeless, and not fit to be a parent. That action was more about the kids' survival than mine. To try and run from my addiction issues, I took off to Nebraska where I dug a larger hole and further hurt my family. Homelessness for me was not eating out of dumpsters. I had friends I mooched off instead. The result was the same for me as for any homeless person—it was the end of my road. Additionally, there are the two separate rollover accidents previously mentioned, during which I was thrown from vehicles and ended up in ditches. Finally, after turning my life around, I have lived through heart failure.

I can say that there have been many pivotal crossroads in my life. I don't think that any of us is different when it comes to crossroads. For me, there were two directions that I was being shown: First, the direction toward ending up like my father: A wife-beating, drunken, little man-child, who never stopped being selfish and narcissistic. He was more of an experience than a person. He taught me negative truths that influenced my values today and showed me a road of hard living and disdain for life. Eventually, his lifestyle killed him. He died an unhappy addict, just as he lived. In his death I found my fork in the road, as I was headed in the same direction. Second, thankfully, I had Mom waving me over her direction, and her road led to "Easy Street" (she literally lives on a street named "Easy"). She helped me trudge forward and inevitably, that road was the one that blessed me with my life as I know it today. I am forever grateful to my mother for the courage she bestowed for me to pave a better road.

Although I look back in amazement at what I lived through, my past doesn't dictate my future, my happiness, or my success. I spent decades building wealth, but I believe my true riches are in my family. I measure my success by the amount of time my kids want to hang out with me and by the friendship I have with each of my grown children. Even if I lose my money, I am not poor today because I have a grandmother, a mother, a stepfather, and a wife, all of whom care about and love me, and honestly, would not be able to get along without me. My riches are not about money— nope, not one bit. Today, my riches come from giving back. Who can I help? Who can I influence? Whose life can I make better?

My legacy includes a lasting impression on my children and my wife. I had that long, awkward talk with my family about my death. It was painful for them, but I will not be truly gone unless they forget me. They will tell their grandkids about me someday. I want it to be a great story! I want their eyes to light up as my kids tell my story. I want them to smile fondly as they talk about my death. That's my legacy! What's yours?

Break It Down

I wrote this book because I kept finding strays who would come to me for business advice. Most of them were younger—18 to 35— but all of them curious as to how I found success. I saw that I was attracting people who were a lot like I was: Most of them had had serious adversity in their lives, but wanted more from themselves. They wanted to own their own business or they wanted to have that killer job. I don't seem to attract formally educated people and my message seems to sink in for those who are aimless and lack purpose but have a lot of motivation. About 90 percent of the time when I speak with a mentee, I quickly learn that they need to be coached on their mindset. Before I could help them with a startup or help them find a great job, I would have to fix their stinkin' thinkin'. I stole that from somewhere, but it literally means they were their own worst enemies. Through coaching, I found a way to break themselves down before anyone else could. Most didn't understand the hard work that it takes to own a business, let alone the perseverance they would need to survive the challenges that go along with being a business owner.

The mentees and I would need to start from the basics, start where I started from—that is, as a newborn in a horrible world full of adversity and haters, all ready to take you out. My mentees would need to build a protective layer of values before they could begin. Having said that, I have built up many mentees to succeed. But the work I am doing is best described as building a loser. We learn most from our failures and experiences within that failure. Training my mentees to see failure as an opportunity is the trick. How do you train someone to be fit to run a company or get that big job, especially when education is not an option? Well, you will see that in this book I am uneducated and highly motivated to succeed, and the businesses I made were done so out of necessity. I cornered myself into being permanently unemployable, by way of adversity. A lengthy criminal record and lack of education comprised my only fuel to show the world I can make it too.

Plan Your Life

This book is by design an effort to teach you not only how to survive adversity but also to use adversity to operate a badass business. I will not show you how to make a business plan; I will show you how to plan your life to run a great business. I will clearly show you how I break down my experiences from childhood to adulthood, combining my life experiences with psychology. I use them as a weapon to run my businesses. Example, you ask? Family in the workplace is very important to me, because it's something I have yearned for, built, and tinkered with in my personal life. Our business is an extension of us! I'm going to extend that to you.

Think of it as a hand up—and if you're in a ditch, you're gonna need it. The good news, though, is that when you find yourself in a ditch, there's nowhere to look—or go—but up.

Your "up" is probably different than mine. My journey is my journey. It's been difficult, as you will soon read. But I wouldn't trade it for anything. I'm not a victim; I'm a victor. Your status as either a victim or a victor, however, is your choice. It will be determined by the values with which you live your life and in whether you are willing to do the hard work to overcome your own "ditch."

You might have read this far, but be thinking to yourself, "I'm not as jacked up as Ron! Why should I keep reading this book?"

My answer is that you should keep reading it before you are as jacked up as I was. Yes, I am a son of a "ditch!" Get it?

This book is not written to be curriculum for any 12-step program—even though, with all of my experience in AA, I could write a good one! It is not a typical self-help book. No, this book is a business book from an overcomer for those who want to overcome their own "ditches."

It's for anyone who wants to become a son (or daughter) of a "ditch" too!

My journey up from that ditch added value to my life because it taught me important values.

I believe a life with values is valuable and adds value to the lives of those with whom you come into contact, the lives of your loved ones, and the lives of the people with whom you work. In this book, I detail the values that I've learned in my journey because I know. . .yes, I KNOW my values can add value to your life, home, and business.

Now, these values (aka, "The Worley Way") are proven. They work. . .if you work them! But I need you to understand that your journey does not need to look like my journey for this book to have value for you. No!

Do I share, in great detail, some of the bad things done to and by me? Yes! But only to do what the typical black velvet background does for that multicarat diamond on display in the jewelry shop: To make the value of the diamond more clearly seen. In this case, the contrast exists to make the values I've learned—and am sharing with you—easier for you to see. And ultimately and hopefully for you to value the values enough to apply them to your life, family, and business. I'm not sharing my past to get your sympathy (I don't need it!), but to inspire you with this one truth: No matter what you are facing, in life, at home, and/or in business, you are not defined by the worst thing you've done or the worst thing that has happened to you. No! You and I are defined by the values we live as we live our lives, love our families, and lead our businesses!

Are we clear?

Are you ready to rise up from your "ditch" and obtain the riches of this life?

Are you ready to become a son (or daughter) of a "ditch?"

Okay, then!

Let's do this!

Riches await!

CHAPTER 2:

WHO I AM WHEN I STOP LYING TO MYSELF

After spending 30 years living in five different states and moving more than a dozen times, I was ready to make real changes and put down some roots. Greeley is where my recovery truly began, and it's where I met Jim Hensel—a man who was going to change my life. I made it to Colorado knowing this stop was the end of the road for me. In my mind, I had two choices: I was going to get sober or I was going to kill myself. I could not stand the piece of crap I had become. I could not envision helping my children live a better life if I stayed this way.

Under my mother's influence, I was given guidance to getting sober. She joined Alcoholics Anonymous (AA) for a short stint and it helped her. A number of times during my many years of drug and alcohol use, she stuck me into AA to try and sober me up, but it never lasted. However, this time was different. I still wasn't even talking to my mother after she essentially told me to "f*ck off." This time, I made the choice on my own to go to AA. I couldn't think of a better place where I could get help.

I was still homeless and living at my brother's house. If I stayed sober, I was welcome there. I didn't have a job yet, so I had a lot of time to go to AA meetings. I went three times a day for 30 days. Ultimately, I was a part of AA for one year. I celebrated my one-year chip and decided to leave the program. I met lots of broken people there—lots of healthy people too. Some people say that addiction is a disease and that willpower does not play a part. I disagree. At the AA meetings, people would talk about alcoholism as a life problem. I treated alcoholism like work. I went to meetings and worked my ass off until the job was done. That part is where willpower comes in. I didn't want to succumb to the AA standard that we all are powerless and forever an addict. I had success by saying that I am never going to drink again. I don't need to justify why I don't drink. I can "recover," rather than "be in recovery" like AA suggests. My work ethic and sheer drive allowed me to be sober by way of AA, but I would be damned if it was going to be a problem for the rest of my life.

Fast forward, eight years of sobriety later, I met Jim through a mutual friend at Gold's Gym. My first thought when I met Jim Hensel was, "Dang, he's a good-looking man!" He was middle-aged, in good shape, confident, and immediately became who I wanted to be when I grew up! I didn't have good male role models when I was younger, so I was intrigued by Jim.

For most of my life, I had put men on a pedestal, from successful business owners to the president of the United States. When I looked at other men, I immediately studied them. I would notice their looks, their hair, the way they dressed or handled themselves, and I would want to be them. I would mimic other men that I hung out with. During my sophomore year of high school, I changed my identity from a pathetic nice guy to a true asshole to women. I started treating them like trash. Why? Because my best friend did, and women seemed to love him. Basically, I stole his identity and used it to get laid. Really, I just didn't want to be me. Instead, I would look at other men and change my persona to be their friend. I would emulate their look and their mannerisms.

Now, I know I was searching for answers to the question, "How can I be a good man?"

Jim and I became business acquaintances through his coaching program "Strength and Honor" and through the store I was managing at the time, Max Muscle. When I first met Jim, he was building an organization to help young men who had overcome struggles to become successful members of society. His own struggles were not of the addiction or abuse variety, but he was a man who overcame serious adversity and lived to tell about it. Jim shared his vision for this effort with me, but I was still struggling with being a good man. So instead of learning from him, I began to think of how I could benefit from this newfound relationship. I began to drown out what he was saying, while daydreaming about different business scenarios in my head. I did this often back then. I treated new friendships like a transaction, and this transaction went nowhere.

We didn't really keep in touch over the next year or so. Then one day, I ran into him at a Pop Warner Football function, where Jim had spoken to the kids. The talk was phenomenal! It was about how young men could grow up with values. After the speech, I went up to talk to him and catch up. I asked to set up a meeting to discuss working together again. A few days later, Jim came over to my house, where we talked further about what he does.

Jim's program, "Strength and Honor," teaches men how to be men, using their own values as their personal code of honor. I originally spoke with Jim to see how he could benefit my company. But as we started talking, I realized that in order to put values in place for the company, I needed to place values in my life. The more I spoke with and worked with Jim, the more I realized I wasn't really okay.

Before we go any further in this book, I want you to answer that question too. Are you okay? Don't lie to yourself. Honesty is the first step to true healing.

I'd been lying to myself for many years. I wasn't okay, and I didn't care. Meeting Jim was an awakening for me. But getting to know Jim Hensel was like seeing myself in the mirror for the first time. The light of his goodness revealed the areas in my life that needed to improve. He made me want to be a better man, and the values he taught me showed me how to do so. For the first time, I saw the power of being good and having values.

I was the child of addicts who became an addict. I'd never seen anyone with true values, and I certainly didn't have any myself. Up to that point, I spent most of my life concerned with what other people thought of me, not what I thought of myself. I had little self-worth. I felt shame. I knew I wasn't okay and didn't know how to fix that...until meeting Jim.

One of the tools that Jim has developed is a challenge for his mentees to write a personal purpose statement for his/her life. Jim calls it an "I AM" declaration. In hindsight, it was the first step in me becoming okay, and it's important to share it with you as we begin this journey together.

I AM

> *My Name is Ron Lloyd Worley—a brave old soul.*
>
> *I am a family man and husband to Erin Brady—the woman I want. I am a father to Payton, Brenden, and Aaron—children I will sacrifice for.*
>
> *I am a guide and caretaker, ready to rescue those in need. I am a man who lives free, fully vested in my values. I commit to make choices and decisions I call "The Worley Way."*

As a child I knew that being a Worley was to be something. My father screamed our last name from the rooftops. He made us understand that we were Worleys and we should be proud.

Worleys were to be feared, not respected. Not a gosh darn person respected my father, not even me. Fear was standard operating procedure in our family. I spent my formative years trying to live up to this expectation. It wasn't until my rebirth into sobriety that I realized that respect is worth much more than fear. Worleys are proud of their name and always carry ourselves in honor of the name.

I believe adults are a product of our childhood. Our parents raise us and try to do better than their parents raised them. They want their kids to have more, do more, and be more. I am no different in that respect. I am a product of my childhood. I had two messed-up parents for much of my youth. Both of my parents were addicts who partied way too much and screwed around with others all the time. . .and right in front of me. They divorced when I was four; they were very young. My dad often thought it was funny to talk about my mother in horrible ways. Dad once told me my mother's vagina smelled like tuna. I was 12 years old. My mom was barely better than dad as an addict, but she cared for us, and her selfishness wasn't quite as deep.

Mom worked hard and provided when she could, but she always had a new man and a new job. Mom raised us with her own guilt from the things she would do the day before or was about to do the next night. We had wants and needs taken care of, but that Atari for Christmas was a babysitting tool, given to us to buy our forgiveness for the countless things that made engaged parents say, "WTF?" Mom was not the mom I always thought I wanted, but eventually I came around to understanding what kind of parent she was. That's what I did to survive. Mom was the best option between the two f*cked-up situations. My parents were like little characters on my shoulders, like an angel and a devil, but each flipping roles back and forth at any given time. You will see in this book that I talk about them both and how each gave me values, but I lead my life more closely to my mother.

Long gone are the days of enforcing fear and having no respect for authority. Instead, I now have total respect for myself and others, and I live within my values. It is my job to carry myself and my actions in a way that displays these values, in order to teach my children and everyone else what it means to be a Worley. My children have learned through my actions how to carry themselves in the community. In turn, the community respects my family.

My children are human, and they are teenagers—they will mess up. What I choose to do about the mess-ups is far different than what my parents would have done. I speak to their heart in a way they can hear me. I lean on our family values and redirect their actions to live within the values. Those methods are how I can guide my children down the path to adulthood. I fully expect them to be adults at 18. I did not become an adult until I was 30, and I had to get there on my own.

Every day in our house is a boot camp towards adulthood. My children are taught well and are treated equally. All of my kids have their own opinions and are formulating their own values; we encourage that and foster discussion around all topics. We didn't learn to trust them until they understood that we were, first, parents living by The Worley Way. Parents first, always. I have never aspired to be their friend but that's what has come out of the process. They know that we trust them until we can't. If they are open and honest about something and come clean right from the start and we find no new facts, then we will help them through the situation. We cannot and will not tolerate any moving truths or gray areas.

I've come to recognize that I take on the role of a rescuer, and with that comes great responsibility. I tend to help others in order to help myself. I have always been a caretaker; the difference is now it has changed from a liability to a responsibility. I don't hand out money to the guy on the corner with a sign—I offer him a job. I spent a lifetime caring for my brothers, sisters, exes, and their kids. That was a liability. Once I figured out that I can be loved and respected by living The Worley Way, I was free.

Right now, I want you to take a few moments before we go any further and write your own "I AM" statement. When writing it, include: Values you represent, people you honor, and describe how you actively live it out. Use my "I AM" statement for an example.

CHAPTER 3:

BRAVERY

> *The Worley Way*—*"Run, don't walk to adversity. I will always be ready to try something new, ready for a challenge with purposeful risk. My heart tells me I will be okay through failure and success. I am naturally brave—it was born in my soul. I will BE brave."*

For my seventh birthday, a friend gave me a shirt that read: "Ft. Lupton Wrestling." I put it on and immediately I felt tough and brave. At that age I didn't understand what brave meant. But I believed I was one badass kid when I wore that shirt. I knew the shirt would make my dad proud too. I would've worn it every day if my mom had let me. Even in her most selfish stupors, she was conscious of my hygiene. Our clothes were always clean. Even our used clothing looked the best it could, but this T-shirt was like Superman's costume for me. DUN DUN DUUUN!

You see very few brave people in this world. Do you know anyone that is truly brave? First responders probably are, for the most part. They wear their Superman costume too. These brave people might make up 5 percent of our population. They run to adversity, danger, and excitement. It's not about the power for them. It's about doing the right thing for society. It's about doing the DUN DUN DUUUN in their costume—and being a hero to others.

Bravery is my favorite chapter. See, without bravery, you will be slaughtered like sheep. We must be lions and willing to hunt at all times. We must be able to take advantage of opportunity, which means that we have to be aggressive and proud; we must be leaders and express our purpose to others. Have you ever seen a sheep do that? Sheep huddle in masses to protect themselves. When predators are on top of them, the sheep huddle up, and the outside of the herd literally is sacrificed for the rest of the herd. In contrast, a lion is a stand-alone warrior, ready to fight at a moment's notice. Alert of its surrounding and cunning but also very much a protector of its pride. That's who we are—brave warriors ready to hunt our next revenue stream or customer or even change our company's model when the times call for those actions. Our pride of lions will follow a fearless leader into anything. Success is earned, not given, and we must fight for it, proud and with purpose.

Image Is Everything

I learned a skill that works for a lot of what I teach: FAKE IT 'TIL YOU MAKE IT. If you are not a brave person, or fear change, or confrontation is not your forte, then you fake it. My "wrestling shirt" was a suit of armor. When I wore it, I felt like a wrestler. I felt I could take on anything. The same is true in my career. In the last 10 years, we've owned multiple businesses: Max Muscle (nutrition and supplement retail chain), Odyssey Builders (real estate holding company), Just Out Services (pretrial services monitoring company), Ron's Bonds (bail bonds), RE Real Estate and Realty One (real estate brokerage firms). When I'm working in real estate, I wear the clothing of a real estate professional. When I go to court for bail bonds, I wear lawyer-type garb. When it's Max Muscle work, I wear a pair of sweats. I make it a point to dress the part.

We had a local bounty hunter who wore all kinds of necklaces and had unbuttoned his shirt three buttons down so his chest was visible. His language was crass and vulgar. It was great for TV, but he also wore that gear when he came to court. Do you think that helped my profession in the eyes of judges? We made a point to change the look of bail in Greeley. We stayed professional, and it worked. We are very well respected by the judges, lawyers, and clientele. I might not be as smart as a lawyer, but I can look as good as one. I can tell you firsthand that people treat me differently when I wear a suit. I am not sure if it's the suit or my confidence in the suit, but does it matter?

As a new agent in real estate, I decided to do the same. I took on the persona of "the bow tie guy." It is my wrestling shirt for the profession. I wear super-hipster suits and a bow tie. I became the high water, cool sock, skinny jean–wearing person I've seen on TV. For the people who knew me, they maybe had a thought or two about my change, but to those who didn't, I looked like a highly knowledgeable agent. When I'm dressing for the day, I always want to be one fashion step above my client. It exudes confidence and breeds success.

When I was a 24-year-old bail agent, the clients and judges always commented about how young I was. What they really meant to say was that they did not respect me. I would overcome their opinion by dressing well and doing my job well. I studied the state statutes, so I was knowledgeable, and I learned the ipso facto bullshito that they used in court. I put on my "wrestling shirt" to be a bondsman. I put on my shirt every time I start something new. It's my bravery cloak. If I hire a young person, I teach them to be really good at two things: To be educated about their job or product and to dress to the hilt (dressed in the very best clothes like they're meeting the president). It's amazing how impressions are affected by both. Unless you're a professional football player or gymnast, as a 24-year-old, people generally do not trust that you have enough experience in whatever profession you're in.

Ask yourself, are you dressing the part? Do you get comments on your style? Compliments are free leads to talk about what you're selling! Last year at our real estate Christmas party, I wore a new suit. I bought the suit just for the event, and it was spectacular. It was blue with three-inch snowmen printed all over it. I had a tie too. Of course, if one is to wear a suit like that, you expect to get comments. Some comments might be good and some bad. By the end of the night, I was a spectacle. At one point, a lady sitting at the table across the room was drunk enough to be brave and come over. She asked me for a picture with her and her friends. Her husband (grumpy old man) took the picture, and I handed her my business card. Three months later, I sold her a house. Bingo!

Let's test out your social response. I want you to go buy the most up-to-date, hipster, popular fashion gear you can find. If you normally wear suits and dresses, then find gear that is more casual. If you are more casual, then buy a suit. Look completely opposite from your usual day-to-day. Be sure to get a new, crazy, fun pair of socks—socks that will gather comments when seen.

Wear your new gear around the office or on your sales calls. Whatever it takes! Every time someone comments on your clothes or those crazy socks, I want you to say, "Thank you, just wearing my work clothes." Be humble, but confident. Watch as strangers ask, "What do you do?" Coworkers will ask if you're looking to get promoted. Conversations quickly grow, and you will be noticed. The effect will help you feel comfortable in the bravery of success. You will find yourself in a leadership role as people will trust you a little more because you look good!

For those of you who are not born brave, or avoid change, or fear the new job, or the unknown, you can put on your wrestling shirt and expose the brave version of yourself. DUN DUN DUUUN!

Determination Is Everything Too

A couple weeks after my seventh birthday party, where I received my DUN DUN DUUUN (wrestling shirt), I joined the wrestling team at the rec center. I needed to match my skills to the shirt I wore. My mom was supportive of this venture and took me to practices and matches three or four days a week. I still remember the first time I walked into the building—a giant metal building located at the middle school. It's still there and is still a wrestling room. It had wall-to-wall mats inside and a stench of man-sweat that permeated from the bodies of dozens of young men. These kids were obviously sweating their balls off, and the coach was yelling about things I had never heard of.

I looked around and saw that many of the kids were in full wrestling gear. I had on shorty shorts, my newly acquired T-shirt and my grungy well-worn old sneakers. At that point in my life, the asymmetry was nothing new: We were poor. I knew it, and I never expected to get all new gear. This time was no different than all of the other sports I had played. When I stepped on the mat for the first time, I looked like a rag-a-muffin—a dirty, unkempt kid (Little Orphan Annie–type).

Quickly, I learned a few basic moves with the coach and my team and knew I was in the right place! I was a skinny, tall, towheaded, white kid in a room full of what I thought were pro wrestlers, by the way they moved around the mat. I was only in second grade, but I looked and acted much older, so the coach thought I was a fourth grader. He put me in the class above my age bracket. I had to wrestle the older kids for weeks before they figured out where I belonged. I felt like the challenge actually helped me. I learned in wrestling that through hard work and bravery, one can always get better. There is an often-used Bible verse that coaches use to motivate their athletes: "As iron sharpens iron, so one man sharpens another" (Proverbs 27:17).

That time in my life made me strong but also helped me meet new people without fear. Those skills were valuable as I changed schools five times in a span of two years. Every new school I attended boiled down to this: I was a poor, white kid everywhere I went, and I had to overcome being the new kid. Wrestling was great for my growing up. It taught me bravery and hard work.

Once I had matches with a few good wrestlers, and beat them, the bullying stopped. I was accepted. Wrestling was my new identity, and it no longer mattered how poor I was or what clothes I wore.

Think of a time when you have been bullied and what you learned from it. Are you stronger today? You can make it a part of your story. Remember, you are brave and victorious because you overcame those times in your life—reasons to be brave in what you do today.

All the outcomes and consequences of your life are teaching moments that build your character. Try to think of the consequences that you endured through your mistakes, or through other people's misconceptions. Think of consequences that might or might not have been your fault (we all make poor choices). In your life today, those consequences were just a blip on the radar and small in comparison but taught you lessons that will stick with you forever.

Part of being brave is acting in the moment to just jump! Imagine you are looking over a 50-foot jump into a lake. You're standing on the edge, and you are trying to decide if you're going to jump. The wind is blowing in your face, and the rocks in the water below look very large from 50 feet above. Fear has encompassed you, and your mind is saying, "walk away." That's when you say, "F*ck it" and jump! When you finally jump, you emerge from the water a hero. You emerge the bravest person alive! Quickly you will forget the fear.

When you're thinking of starting that new business, say, "F*ck it" and jump! That's the jump-off point we all experience—when you are about to make a choice but a little fear consumes you. All of the what-ifs begin to surface: "What if I fail, what if____, what if____?" I say, "F*ck it" and jump! Life's consequences are inconsequential to your character. Nothing compares to being bullied or walking into a room full of wrestlers as the new kid. You can rectify virtually any choice you make in life and in business because you are brave enough to fix it.

Such times can make or break you. In those moments, you have to make a choice and deal with the consequences that come. That decision is what makes a leader—bravery. These "f*ck it" moments are riddled throughout business. We come to a crossroad daily. We can't sit back and wait or linger to let the issue work itself out—we must bravely make a choice!

Before you jump, you need to eliminate some of the associated risk. It's easy to be brave when you are confident and have low risk. I'll talk more about confidence in the next chapter, so for now, just know it's time to jump.

I use these bravery values in my life today. I do not allow myself to be normal, or mediocre—I want to stick out like a sore thumb! I want to be the crazy, outgoing guy everywhere I go. I'm not afraid to try new things or introduce something new in my company. I can be brave and trust myself.

You cannot be successful without bravery. Make that phone call you don't want to make. Take that meeting you really wanted to avoid. Write down a few moments that stick in your memory where you wish you did something instead of nothing. Consider if this issue is something you can still fix today. Ask yourself if it happens again, can you bravely choose a different way to handle it?

Unwavering Bravery Isn't Physical Fighting

When my brother, Les, and I were young, maybe seven and nine years old, we fought a lot, as brothers do. Our fights were physical, but we never accomplished anything. We never really went blow for blow up to this point. One day, my dad just about had enough. He took us outside and said we were going to finish it once and for all. He drew a 20-foot circle in the dirt driveway with the heel of his boot. Dad stuck us in the middle of the ring and told us not to come out until one of us dropped. His order meant that we were to kick the crap out of each other. I couldn't beat him up for real! Usually our fights were my trying to present dominance, not hurt him. I can't say the same for Les. I would frustrate the hell out of him when we fought. I was bigger and stronger, and he couldn't win.

Les brought his anger when the fight started! He was so pissed, he came swinging. I tried to mess around and throw punches without hurting him, but he came so hard and ended up landing one straight on my nose. I got mad! I threw a barrage of punches and landed a few too. Dad would yell at us to swing and pushed us back into the circle when we came out. Unless one of us dropped, there was no quitting.

Eventually, Les tired out, and the punches were too much. He collapsed in the middle of the ring. God, I felt awful! Les showed the most bravery that day. He kept coming at me until he was exhausted. This fight did not establish a pecking order, and the fights kept on. He earned my respect a few years later, when he laid me out with a golf club. He knocked me clean out of the back of the pickup we were fighting in. I knew then that he might not be as big as I was or as strong but his bravery was unwavering.

But while I saw bravery during a physical altercation in my childhood, I discovered that true bravery didn't come from fighting. It came from getting away from that lifestyle as an adult. It was teaching my children to be kind and to not fight—putting an end to the vicious cycle! Sometimes, especially in business, it is best to do nothing—we must take the high road. It takes a brave person to do nothing. Before you react, stop and think, then decide what response aligns with your values. If someone writes something nasty or something you don't agree with, don't react ... enact. Enact your values! Everyone has emotions, but you need to learn how to harness them to make wise business decisions.

The ring that my dad drew with his boot in that driveway was a constant reminder that I could fight my way out of anything. In wrestling, there is a ring to keep the wrestlers fighting (wrestling) in a contained area. Fighters in MMA have an octagon, and boxers have a square ring. I'm a wrestler, so I most relate to that moment before the match when I'm in my stance across from my opponent. My stomach has butterflies, I feel like I have to poop, and all I want to do is get out of the ring. But first, I must whoop this guy's ass! What's funny is in that moment, I would actually notice the other wrestler's shoes. I would base their skill level off how nice their shoes were ... I digress. I am a warrior, and I have been sent into a ring to fight the other school's warrior, and neither of us can come out of the ring until one of us wins. We always want to be the winner!

The ring is the place to take your issues and your hardships—take them to the ring and battle with them. Make no mistake, we all have adversity to battle. The ring is where we fight. We use whatever means in the ring to be victorious over adversity. Bring a gun to the knife fight. Bring your shield and your spears. I don't care, just bring it! We need to fight any way we can in order to win. It's your life, and it's time to be okay with all those things that have "happened to you." Every problem I had in the past, every old, nasty, negative recording, everything negative anyone ever told me, all went to the ring to be battled, and I slammed that shit in the head with a fire axe tipped with poison drops. I overcame it at all costs!

We fight our issues and hardships in the ring, not in public and not with other people. We fight our issues in the safety of our ring. The ring is also for the safety of others. I used to let my issues control me and the way I acted towards others. If I was angry, everyone took the brunt. Now, I fight my anger in the ring so it doesn't affect others.

As an adult, I spent five years ridding myself of my issues and bringing them to the ring. My ring was counseling. It was a place where I could hash out all the issues that I acquired through the unhealthy life I had lived. My psychiatrist was there to listen but also to give me feedback and reveal truths about myself. It required me to do the work. AA was another ring for me and I also used the gym as my ring space. I worked out a lot! It was active meditation and a great tool to fight those demons.

Your ring might be different from mine. Some people might just need a block of time; others drive their cars and talk to themselves. Today, when I have to work through something, my ring is either the theater room or my office. I will throw on a movie and go to work, or if I really need space, I will go to my office after hours and "do work" battling against that adversity.

I have since reprogrammed my thoughts and replaced old negative recordings that played in my head with new positive recordings. These new recordings fuel great successes in my businesses today. Bravery is about being able to face your adversity with wisdom.

Use your ring as a place to take your adversity and fight it out. Take five negative things that you say to yourself and write them in the ring. Write down five more incidents that have caused pain or struggle and continue to come up today. Finally, write five things that people say about you that you don't like. Put it all in the ring, and then battle it there.

Adversity never ends; we just need a process to deal with it. The process is to place the adversity in the ring, battle it, and leave it in there until you need to fight it again. By committing to battling adversity in the safety of the ring, you normalize your day-to-day behavior. You will pause before you react. You allow yourself to deal with the issue in the ring, rather than reacting to the issue in the moment.

If our issue or hardship is with another person, it is reparable. We can make amends if we wronged someone—apologize and promise never to harm that person again. We need to be able to move on from things with a heart of forgiveness, including forgiving yourself. Take your adversities and wrongdoings and put them in the ring, battle them out, make amends, and then forgive.

If you're like I am—a believer in God—or are religious, you probably grasp that concept. I put my issues in the ring, fight them out, make amends, and then give it to God. Once God has it, I no longer own the issues or take them back. We let time put distance between them, and we move on. The ring becomes a protective place for all your skeletons. No longer are they secrets, or guilt, or shame—they are in the ring forever. We battle them out and then move on! In a 12-step program, the expression "Let Go and Let God" reminds us to admit our wrongdoings and let go. When I make a mistake, it goes in the ring where I can battle it out and build wisdom.

It is easy to try something new, or out-of-comfort-zone ideas, if the only consequence is that you have to put something in your ring. Fear is an illusion created by consequences. If you can remove the consequence, it removes the fear. Now, you can bravely open that business, or fire that employee, or take out that loan.

Instead of the fear of consequences, I want you to start saying, "What if it works? What if I'm successful?" Make a plan, build your systems, and try it—whatever "it" is. If you want to skydive, try it. If you want to start a company, try it. Prove to yourself that you are capable by setting mini goals and achieving them. Literally write down your new recording—what success means to you. Write down positive affirmations toward those successes. Remember, f*ck it—try it! The point is to have recordings that increase positivity for you. They are very personal and private, so say whatever you like!

CHAPTER 4:

CONFIDENCE

__The Worley Way__—"I really am what you see. I am genuine. I will not pretend to be or be anybody other than I am. I have connected my brain with my heart, and I like my heart. I am sure that my intentions are good. I am sure that I will fix the mistakes that I make. I am sure I can live, decide, and choose based on my values. I am sure my emotions will not control me. I am sure I will face adversity daily, and I am sure I will continue to face it head on. I am transformed. I am sure about myself."

I often stop and analyze myself and why I might do things. There are two questions I ask:

How well am I following my values?

How is the wisdom from my past influencing how I operate in life and business today?

As a young man, I lacked confidence. I was an addict, and it's hard to be confident when you're homeless and on drugs. No one trusts someone like that.

Today, I am not homeless, and I have great wisdom in the subject of confidence. As I mentioned before, I practiced five years with a professional to get my confidence. After that, I asked myself, "How did I do that?" How did I go from not a shred of confidence to being able to teach someone else to have it? There are three parts to it: preparation, persistence, and practice.

Preparation

I grew up playing football. We would practice all week to be ready for the big game. We worked hard to know the other team's plays, and we would run those plays against our team, over and over all week. The same should be true with your business. I don't prepare by building a business plan, forecasting sales and expenses first. I prepare by writing up the values that define my business. Bravery, Confidence, Freedom, Hard Work, Trustworthiness, Wisdom, Positivity, Friendship, Family, and Happiness (i.e., The Worley Way) are the values that I use in every business I start and run. I then make three new values that pertain specifically to the new company. I promote these three values to the employees and the public. These three new values are the core of the business and are not to be confused with personal values, which are my 10 values above. Those 10 are just mine and are used to run all my businesses.

Once I have defined my three new values and they are in place, I can move forward right off the bat with the right people, places, and systems based on those values. If I'm interviewing potential employees, it's important to know how my values match up with theirs and vice versa. Does the interviewee even have any? Prepare and research, but start with values.

Now, what? How do you prepare your business or your department to not only have values but also to build the company culture to use your values?

1. I like to build marketing material and company policies to help promote them. I'll build social media material to post

and create posters to hang in the business. I will also add the business values to the policy manual and to employee-hiring collateral. You can see examples on my website. (www.ronworley.com). When a new hire comes into my business or a customer visits, I want my values poster to be the first thing they see. I'll hang that puppy right on the front door. I'll promote the values on receipts, and I'll even make business cards that include them. The point is that I want everyone in the building to see them and eventually know them. Customers will ask about them; employees will be reminded of them daily.

2. Coach your employees. When speaking to an employee, use values to correct behavior, or to inspire and motivate. Much like I do with my children, I will boast and proudly explain our values to employees upon hiring. I will add them to the job description that they will go over with me and sign when hired. I will go over the company policies and will point out our values. And when they have stepped over a line, I will coach them back into line using the values to do so.

   For example, if an employee isn't doing their "chores" after their shift, I will explain to them the value or values they are breaking as well as the people their behavior affects negatively. It sounds too simple, right? It is—that is the beauty of it. (Note: this will not be the only time you hear this from me because I am a transformational owner, not a transactional owner.)

3. Lastly, I will speak to outside people about our business using our values. Question from the community: Who are you and what does your company do? Answer: We are a tech company that _____ (from the I AM Statement, reflecting the business), we believe in _____ (values

1-3), and we promise to _____ (from the WE WILL Statement). How do you identify these statements, you ask?

- I AM statement: This is a statement that explains how you use your values in your business. You will want to use yours in the statement. For example, we are ABC Tech, and we use our **wisdom** to influence our **community** and **aid** in their personal lives. The three values of ABC Tech are wisdom, community, and aid.

- WE WILL statement: This statement is used to explain how you will achieve your values for your clientele/ employees. For example, we promise to use our technology to increase your database of customers in your community. Our attention to detail is matched only by our wisdom in the industry gained after over 20 years. Our customer service is second to none as we work hard to assist you in all matters tech.

Preparation lowers risk and makes you confident in your decision to start a company or interview for a new job. I have never opened a company with less than 100 percent confidence. In your preparation and forecasting, first think about three things:

1. What problem am I solving?
2. Does this uphold my values?
3. Can I be purposeful with it?

In preparing for my first company, I was told to build a SWOT Analysis (Strengths, Weaknesses, Opportunities, and Threats) and a business plan. WTF! Is that right? Yeah, I said the same thing, and frankly I didn't feel smart enough to build them.

Furthermore, the purpose of this book is not to help you write a SWOT Analysis or business plan. As I wrote in Chapter One, the purpose of my book is to prepare you by teaching you values that can make your life, your family, and your businesses extraordinary! As you learn, live, and lead with the values in this book, you will build confidence both in yourself and in those you're leading as you build your life, family, and/or business.

But I'm getting a little ahead of myself.

Before we get too much into what you're building, let's first look at how you are building what you want to build, lest I assume you're more prepared than you actually are.

Assumptions Can Be the Enemy of Preparation

If you assume you already know how to do something, then you are more apt to neglect—or just ignore—the preparations normally necessary for success with whatever that "something" is in your life.

It's so true: there are no shortcuts to true success.

Since my wife, Erin, and I had already learned that the hard way, we were more prepared for success when we decided to open a sports nutrition business.

One of the biggest mistakes in business is assuming that if you build it, they will come. When we were opening Max Muscle, my wife and I knew the only way to find customers was through guerilla marketing, which is a tactic utilizing unconventional strategies to promote products or services. Guerilla marketing often relies on personal interaction and has a smaller budget. We had to premarket by way of the community. We went out to the gyms and to events, such as races, and handed out samples of our product. We held parties with friends and invited them to sample and test our products. Everywhere we went, for 10 months straight, we were talking about our business.

Once we started premarketing, we were basically selling products out of the garage, but people wanted to see what we had, so I invited one of Erin's friends over to take a look at our products. I set up a display of everything we had in stock (in the garage) and attached product data sheets to them. On her way over, she told me she was bringing four more friends with her. When all five of them arrived, I had made them each little bags of samples and inserted our business cards into the gift bags with tissue paper. I mixed up shaker cups of protein flavors for them to try and gave them fat burners right as they walked in. Within 15 minutes into the tasting, they were buzzed up on fat burners and feeling goooood! In that hour, I sold $1,600 in product and sent them home with more samples to try. It was a good sale before we even opened, and we knew we had just found a big piece of our market—women! We knew who would be coming into the store and why they would come see us over our competition—all well before the first product was officially sold. We eliminated most of our risk by preparation in the marketplace, and we had presales.

Our efforts in the preparation allowed us to have a $2,500 soft-opening day. We had a great week, which led to a great month. In three months, we were topping the leader boards for the entire franchise. Our momentum from the premarketing and preparation sprang us into owning three more stores, and eventually selling all the stores and becoming millionaires. Preparation is very important!

You can implement those tactics in any job, sales, or business. As an employee, you might take a product out on the road and get it in front of people to increase your sales. Or you might go to events with a booth or volunteer to get your name out there. It will be hard work (another value of The Worley Way), but if you hang in there, you will have a wonderful test market and a boatload of confidence in your company or product before you open. We took negative comments and learned how to educate the customer about our product by the time we finally opened the doors.

Education certainly is a key component in preparation. But education doesn't look the same for everyone, and that's okay. I was told that going to college would get you a great job. Of course, nobody mentioned what happens when you get kicked out ... twice.

I was a horrible student and used school as a social arena or a place to get dates. I had a lot of fun in school, but I didn't learn a damn thing, which hurt me in many ways. I sought help writing this book because I can't conjugate a verb to save my life. I struggle with reading too. I hate it, and most of the time when I read, I lose track of the words within minutes or fall asleep.

But all is not lost. I learned and still learn so much from podcasts, interviewing others, and watching video blogs. Whatever it takes for you to educate yourself, just do it.

I opened a real estate brokerage only 10 months after I started practicing real estate. I won't share the name here but it was local to Greeley. The state of Colorado at the time required two years as an active agent before you could open a brokerage. That wasn't my goal, and that obstacle wasn't going to work for me, and with help, we found a way to bypass that barrier. Erin and I made it a race to finish our testing to get our license, and in one short month we passed our tests. Usually it takes agents a minimum of six months to get licensed. We quickly employed our marketing machine, and started getting and closing deals. Within three months, we had shared 10 deals. We learned fast!

The whole point for my getting into the real estate business wasn't to do deals. It was to own a brokerage. You might ask why that objective was the point? We found it difficult to work for other people, being one reason; as for the second reason, we like to have our own brand, and the ability to grow and scale into our own revenue streams. I do not like paying for other people's dreams and toys. In fact, we passed up working with a few different brokerages because our friend and soon-to-be partner wanted us to work with him right from the beginning to help open a brokerage.

I knew nothing about running, starting, or owning a brokerage. We were in mega-learning time, and I was a sponge soaking up everything anyone would teach. The main thing that gave me confidence is that our brokerage partners were veterans and knew a lot about the real estate business. With the addition of my skill level in business and Erin's skills in marketing, we knew we would be great.

In the first six months, we acquired 30 agents, and we haven't put another dime into the business since our original investment. It works!

I educated myself on the market, the competition, and the product—those are easy. The hard part is knowing that wisdom only comes from doing. As in my case with the real estate brokerage, I could never have done it without someone else who had the wisdom in real estate. We partnered up with the two people we knew and had brought us into the industry. Again, no names here. Both partners had 30 years' experience between them. One of the new partners was the bullshitter (he had the gift of gab), and he did a lot of deals a year based solely off his ability to BS. I loved that ability and looked up to him as a mentor. The other partner was the most experienced at 20+ years. She was the cooler head and showed us that you can love your clients as well as make money on them. Neither had any ability to run a business. Neither knew how to start one, let alone maintain one or grow one.

Mr. BS had to convince partner B to go into the brokerage business, and it was tough doing so. B saw the potential in failing instead of succeeding. Maybe she saw the writing on the wall before it was written. Eventually, they both saw the value of us in the business realm, and we agreed to open. Erin and I had been running Max Muscles for eight years with major success, and our reputation preceded us. This venture was not retail. The difference would turn out to be gigantic.

At this point in the relationship, figuring out who was the best fit to do what was very important. We decided our new partners would be the managing brokers because they had the experience and met state requirements. Erin handled marketing, and I was operations. We made clear roles for each. The business was in all of our names, but both partners were registered as managing brokers to satisfy the state. We were off to the races.

I'm not afraid to fail. I have failed many times before and have grown from those failures. I have lost businesses. I have lost many, many personal battles. I speak about some of them in this book. My years as a wrestler and growing up fighting in the streets taught me how to lose and come back stronger. I use my failures as motivation to succeed. I use failure as determination to prove to some imaginary person inside myself that I am worthy of success. I am my own worst enemy, and failure can be twisted into sabotage and hatred of oneself, especially if you battle with low self-esteem. I chose to change my thoughts about failure into being a positive rather than a negative. It's not the end. It's the beginning.

"I have not failed. I've just found 10,000 ways that won't work."
— **Thomas A. Edison**

I am not saying, don't jump off the cliff! I'm saying make the jump a little less intimidating by being confident in the landing. Prepare for the landing. First, do your homework, and be knowledgeable and wise about the landing. What are you jumping into? In the business realm, what kind of industry? What research can you do about the industry? Finally, what documents can you build to support your landing? Budgets, pro-forma business plans all are good examples. Study the potential results and possibilities for failure. Those steps are the heart of risk-taking.

Second, know the landing area. Prepare for the landing before you jump. Don't wait until you're in the air falling to your certain death. We are not going to open a business without understanding all the revenue streams, customer acquisitions cost, employee retention rates, cost of goods, etc., etc.

Third, reduce the options of failure by planning the results in an actionable "what's next?" scenario. We want to prepare ourselves for the uncertainty of the landing. If you open and no customers walk through the door, what are you going to do? If you have customers, but the cost of goods or manufacturing skyrocket, what are you going to do?

Erin and I opened our first Max Muscle Store in 2010, not a great time to open as the economy was not great. We had great margins on protein, and we were making money. After a few months in business, the price of protein skyrocketed by triple the costs. We no longer had the convenience of making money on proteins. We couldn't raise the price to match the triple hike, as our customers would find cheaper protein. We decided to raise the price by $10, which was a third of the increased cost. At that point, we were making $17 per tub of protein. After we weighed the cost of the employee who sold it, and all the bills to keep the business open to sell that protein, we were -$5 per tub. We decided that we would need to sell another, more profitable product with the protein. Something with a higher margin. So we took our vitamin, attached it to the protein, and sold them together. We hiked the price of the protein up by adding the value of the vitamin. The vitamin cost us $11 but sold for $32. So we gave the combo a $90 price tag, and sold them all day long. The consumer would save $10 for the two products; for us, we upped our average sale and margin into a profitable landing for our jump into the nutrition industry.

Persistence

As a child, I grew up around abuse and trauma, and witnessed more than I should have. Before age 12, I witnessed sexual abuse, drug abuse, and smoked weed weekly, or whenever my father would allow me to. I witnessed countless beatings that my father gave to his girlfriends, friends, and us children. My dad also beat the dogs regularly. I watched my mother be beaten several times by one of the many men she dated. To top it all off, we were in the tail end of the Cold War, and I was worried sick that the United States was going to be blown off the map by a USSR nuclear bomb.

I think those factors were why I wet the bed. I wasn't a confident child. I wore ugly clothes, spoke crassly, and had a family that reminded me of the Beverly Hillbillies. Peeing in the bed didn't help. I genuinely thought I was a failure by the time I was seven or eight years old. I looked for the bad in myself, and my only reprieve was sports.

Peeing in the bed became a nightly fear and a daily embarrassment every single day until I was 12 years old. At that age, the driving force in my life was normalcy. In my household, there wasn't any semblance of normal—from the actual house, to our clothes, to my mom's job. I held onto the feeling that I was a constant burden for my mom. She worked a 15-hour day "man's job," then came home to two kids and figured out how to put a roof over our head, food on the table, and clothes on our backs. I knew the struggle she felt every day even at a young age. I would have moved heaven and earth to make things easier for her. The constant need to change the sheets weighed heavily on me, as one more task for mom to do every day. The ever-daunting thought that one more time of washing sheets could be the thing that sent her to the bar instead of coming home was suffocating for me. If for some reason I didn't pee in the bed the night before, I still lived in angst of going to bed the next night because I knew it was just a matter of time.

Staying the night at a friend's house was the worst of all. Usually, my mother forewarned my friend's parents and asked them not to tell my friend. I can remember waking wet and having to tell my friend's mother that I peed in the bed. I would do so before my buddies would wake up. At Derek's house, my best friend at the time, I woke to a puddle one morning. I tried to hide it from him. I couldn't get to his mom before he realized my darkest secret. He made fun of me, and for the first time, I was confronted with my problem on a public level. That following Monday, kids at school found out, and I heard the torment for several weeks.

My mother tried everything to stop it. I couldn't help but wonder if she truly was sad for me or embarrassed of me. I choose to believe the first one.

Mom invested in an alarm that hooked to a pad that I kept under my sheets on the bed. When the pad felt wet, it would sound the alarm. I was a top-bunk kid and when that God-awful noise sounded, it would break me from my slumber and send me into panic. I would scream and bawl, and even fell off the bed numerous times before mom got rid of that damn thing. We even watched a movie about a boy who peed in the bed on the Lifetime channel in hopes to learn something. We coined the movie's title as, "The runaway boy who peed in the bed." Though I made fun of the movie, I truly identified with the boy. It helped me to realize there were others in the world like I was. I mean, shit! They made a movie about it! We concluded that my problem was emotional.

But what was the cause? I believe trauma from my mom's household had something to do with my wetting the bed. I had so much stress and pressure of being an adult at Mom's. When my mom moved to Wyoming, and my parents were separated for the first time, their fighting stopped! And, like a switch turning off, when I moved into my dad's house full-time, the bed-wetting stopped. I felt safe and at ease for the first time in my life.

Even though it was temporary, it felt nice. Dad was a very abusive man to his women, but to us boys, his boys, he was soft-hearted most of the time. That could change in an instant, of course, and next thing you know, he would have me flat on my back in a chokehold. Dad led with power. He was 5'6" and strength just beamed from him. He would be triggered by little things and fought anyone who crossed him.

Dad was an alpha male, and like an alpha dog, he kept his litter in line. He was constantly nipping and barking at us to correct our behavior, but all the while we knew he would protect us from harm. I felt safe from the world with dad. I felt strong and powerful. He was proud of the Worley clan, and I spent my entire life trying to make him prouder. The strength in that entire concept can't be lost on you. Dad was a bad leader, but still a leader, and his litter was his to protect, love, and leave when he decided. He completely wrecked his kids mentally, but all of us became great fathers. I repeat that fact to you: each of us became great leaders of our litter.

What does bed-wetting have to do with persistence? It's because I lived through it for many, many years with only hope as an answer. My mother lived it with me, and she persistently tried everything. That dedication is what I meant when I said my mother was less selfish than my dad. Mom invested money and a lot of her time in my bed-wetting problem. She made it her problem too. We kept trying and trying. I didn't have a choice whether I wet the bed or not each night, and nothing I did could make it stop. I had to endure and persevere through many wet nights, horrible embarrassment, and lots of trial and error, but we kept on trying. Mom was teaching me confidence in that bad moment of my life, but I didn't realize that lesson until much later. She was setting me up to be a businessman by teaching me to throw all you got at the issue and just keep going.

Growth of your business or even growth as a leader is dependent on persistence. You want to lead your team with consistency and persistence. As a start-up company, the opening of your business is like drinking water from a 55-gallon drum. So much needs to get done, most of it is new to you, and all of it is stressful. Opening day of the real estate brokerage was a barrage of agents and their issues. That onslaught would not be an issue normally, but all were computer and software issues. I was responsible for hooking all of them up to the software systems, printers, and I was responsible for building the on-boarding and training sites. My background? Not computers. But I was the only one of the four of us business partners that could even grasp the systems, so I had to do it. I spent months in preparation, learning by failures, and I copied a lot of what I'd seen others do in other brokerages within the franchise. I was able to build on-boarding systems that worked great. We on-boarded 35 people in six to eight months. Each one got easier and easier as we went along. With the first few, I would get super stressed out and start sweating, and inside my mind, I was super frustrated. Nothing worked as it should, and I had to problem-solve every single time. I persevered and didn't let the agents see me sweat. After 10 agents or so, I had perfected the systems and knew the issues that might come up. I learned to onboard remotely, so I didn't have to be problem-solving in person, and agents felt more at ease with the lesser fix time in the systems.

Every single company or system is the same thing. Drink from the 55-gallon drum and just keep working and perfecting your systems. Eventually, you're drinking from a glass, and you're dry as a bone. We have to do the work and solve the problems. I don't care who you are or how much experience or education you have, you cannot anticipate all the woes of startup. You just jump in and work hard and keep fighting toward one successful task after another. You will lose money, and you will fail at some things, but if you win enough battles, you will win the war.

Practice

I do all the traditional training methods like role-playing, company meetings, and one-on-one performance reviews. That's only half of it. I don't look to have the perfect transaction with a customer, or the highest sale, or even a nice review. What I practice at the heart is how to connect to our purpose. I connect to the value of my businesses.

In bail bonds, we use the value "compassion." I align myself to compassion every single time I deal with a customer. True, 25 years of hearing every sob story known to the human race has caused me to be callous to people at times. When someone tells me why they can't pay me or goes on about how they got such a raw deal by the police, I tend to tune out and say something in return like, "Oh, that is horrible."

These protective walls make the person think I'm listening, but they also are protecting me from falling into their drama. You would be surprised how much manipulation I can see in one day. In a single week, we will bail people out of jail, yes, but also we have homeless people and strays off the streets who will come into the office for help. I think we are the middle ground from the professionals in the court systems and the streets of Greeley. We will have victims of domestic violence come in to find help or homeless people needing to take a break.

We once had a lady come into the office and use our bathroom and stayed in there for 45 minutes, and when she finally emerged from throne, she had scrubbed the entire bathroom sparkling clean. My compassion for people in their various situations is the purpose of our business: We are there to help with anything we can. In return, I get 90 percent referral business. "Call Ron, he will help." That recommendation is what I hear daily. It makes my heart happy each and every time because I know we are in line with our core values.

I assess if I'm headed in the right direction in my life, at my businesses, and in my jobs. My values are important to keep me purposeful and focused. I try to transform people with every transaction, and it takes practice. I want each transaction to feel effortless for my clients. I walk them through an experience of our business rather than just sell them on something. This approach is easy to do with a few questions about themselves. Be entertained by their story, and then fill the needs from that story.

Each company is different, but values are values, and if your company or your job can connect to the customers' values, connect to who they are, then you are transforming their lives. I can't count how many times I have helped someone find a place to get sober, or counseling, or a place to stay. I can't tell you how many people I have helped lose weight or change their lives through health.

Even in real estate, we can be transformational by switching our focus from the commission to values. One of our values is "home" and within the definition of home, commission isn't a part of it. When we show a property, clients get an experience from start to end, from bringing toys for their kids while we are showing houses, to cool pictures of them in front of their new home holding a "sold sign," which we post for them on social media to celebrate with their friends. Each time we put the client under our wing, they are transforming within our process of defining the customer's values.

If I have a big deal to close, or am meeting my in-laws for the first time, I want to approach those meetings the same way. I want them to get to know me quickly and love the crap out of me. I have practiced that behavior for many years. As a young man growing up, I yearned for that attention. I lacked self-esteem, as you might have already guessed by now. Hand-me-downs from Goodwill, uncut hair, and holes in my shitty shoes were fine for a nine-year-old, and frankly I didn't even care until I was 12 years old. That's when I contracted warts all over my hands, which really seemed to disgust the girls at my school. My entire sixth-grade year, I didn't realize I was supposed to brush my teeth, and didn't. Imagine that! I met a girl who didn't care about my warts and clothes, and she made me brush my teeth. I felt amazing because I could hold hands with her after school every day. She was also my first French kiss. Rachael was her name, and she filled the void of no mother in my life at that point. Of course, we broke up soon enough, but Rachael had created a new Ron Worley. I still wore ragged clothing and my hair was never cut, but I had found a way to feel good about myself. Girls!!!!

As I grew into a man, and after many women, divorces, and literally countless one-night stands to fill the motherless hole in my self-esteem, I had gotten sober and had gotten a fix on my life through counseling. I realized that business, and especially sales, was a lot like landing a beautiful woman. I am not being sexist here, though. I actually have quite a healthy outlook on women these days, but I had to learn the rules of attraction. You have to remember I was raised by a womanizing, woman-beating, careless leader of a man: my father.

So how is dating like business?

- In any dating realm, you must attract the other person. I am specifically speaking personally here, not as in business, although the analogies are the same. We must always dress the best, and I will cover that in other chapters. We must speak to them as if they were the only one in our lives. A good sale wants all the attention in the room. We are not trying to one-night-stand the sale but rather caress it into the long-term relationship. I use humor to attract customer/sales/girlfriends. I find areas in the conversation to input my humor but also show my confidence. I lead them into conversations that will shed a little light on my own life, where I will share snippets to gain their trust.

Give trust, get trust. If you are meeting the parents for the first time—or clients, to keep it relatable here—you only want them to see enough of your inner thoughts to know they can trust you.

- Relate, relate, relate! To the parents, I would relate to their lives at their ages. Talk taxes, politics, educations, etc. Imagine a little 15-year-old boy coming over and changing the oil with the old man of his girlfriend on the first date. That one won me huge points. Today, it's values that I relate to, like how I raise my kids, or how the country might be falling apart, and how "kids these days" could learn a thing or two. Those subjects tend to start conversations that lead to trust and likability. First, no one today wants to admit that the people younger than they are are doing it better. Second, they are willing to expose their thoughts on how they could or did do it better. All kinds of common ground in these conversations.

- Always be closing. Yes, it's cliché, but circling around my objective is something I would always do when I met a girl that gave me butterflies. I was always leading them back to dating me. I think the kids these days call it "talking," which for me always led to the goal that I was looking for to fill that void in my heart. In business or sales, we are filling the void of revenue.

I even have a few lines that I use to get things going. Over time and with practice, you will too. Here is the secret to the in-laws loving me and landing the big deal—I sell myself! Seriously, I have to practice at being myself, letting down walls, and offering little pieces of my life in order to soften my appeal. I like to tell stories, and of course, I am conscious of the room. I'm not going to tell dirty jokes to my in-laws, right? I tell my in-laws anecdotes about the way I was raised, or about my parents and their lives. I make a connection to their hearts using myself as the fall guy. When I open up to them with a story, I am showing them that I trust them with that little piece of me.

How do you get to that place? How do you get comfortable with sharing your story? This stage might take years for some, and it did for me. I am an attention-seeking whore and love to shock the hell out of people. That's me now. I spent 29 years embarrassed of who I was and where I came from. Over time, I built small wins in my life. Got sober, made some money, bought a house, bought another house, bought a mansion, and voilà! *Ditches to Riches* was born. Not as easy as it sounds, but that's the short story.

This book is the long story. When I tell my story, it isn't a story of my past, it's a story of my success. I arose from the literal ditch to become a leader in business, which allows me to speak about my past without letting it define me. I am personal friends with a congressmen and lawyers and judges. Some of those judges sentenced me in the past, and none of them hold it against me. I don't like to brag about my successes, so I'd rather tell you how to get yourself to the point of selling your story. Let's take you there.

Let's create your story. Write down the following on something to diagram or go to my website for the tools.

- **Where was I?** Tell the story of your past. Write it all down. Let it soak in, and own it. This is your fuel to go forward. You might not use it all, but you want bullet points that got you to this point that drove you to buy this book. You can write a book some day and tell it all. No one wants your complete story in a first meeting. I put mine on our business website. I went for it.
- **Where am I now?** Talk about your successes. This element is more personal than business. How many kids you have, awards you have received, businesses you own, etc. This section is not a place to talk about your material possessions—no cars, no boats, none of that BS. My

introduction to speaking at events is as a family man who is an author, artist, and businessman.

- **How did I get here?** This part is the most beneficial. I speak about the things I did to fix myself first, then talk about the success I have had. This area is where my values come into play. My identity is that of my values, which guide me to my successes. What are yours?

Now, wrap it all together, and that's your story. When you speak of your past, let your "today" make you proud of yourself. I am so free to tell my story because I am not my past. You are not either, and it makes us super-interesting and real to the consumer. Your clients and bosses will be able to relate to your story rather than what they see in front of them. You can now be vulnerable but safe. You can tell a story in a relatable way because you no longer are that person but rather a valuable person of values and success.

The truth is, I have no shame about my past, so it's easy to trust people with it. In return, it is natural for people to open up to me. At that point, trust is built. Neither of us is going to share something truly secret, but it's a step in that direction. This juncture is also why it is super-important to rely on your values. They are great talking points and a great way to back yourself up. I can't count how many times I have said to a customer, "I can't do that because my values won't let me." Practice your values and practice *being* them. Confidence will follow.

I am authentic at this point in my life, and my companies are too. I didn't just wake up one day being earnest and real. I practiced it. I had to say and do things that felt uncomfortable at first. It took me eight years of sobriety before I owned my addictions in public. When I came out with my story, it made me real. People respected me. Today, I tell my story to anyone I can, and it's not scary anymore.

Telling your story sets you up to deal with all aspects of

discomfort. A lot of uncomfortable situations will come up in business. You will have to fire someone, you will lose money, and you will be embarrassed at some point.

Firing my first person was god-awful. It's one of those times when you have to just rip off the Band-Aid; you have to get in the mindset that it's part of your job to fire them. That said, the first person who I fired cried, and I felt horrible. I even gave her a hug after. I apologized for her being the problem. That's how I dealt with the discomfort. I made it my problem. I learned from that experience, and from then on I would just walk into the meeting and say, "Hey, we are letting you go. I need your keys and your uniforms. Here is your last check. Thank you for your service to us." I never gave a reason or allowed them to make excuses. It's already done before I walked in.

I actually have a huge fear of confrontation that stems from every confrontation ending in a fistfight. So my fear of going back to jail paralyzes me in confrontation. I had to change that effect to be a real owner of my companies. The moment that confrontation begins, my fight or flight kicks in, and I lose all thought—thus, why I lost every fight with every women ever. If I can't physically correct an altercation, then I'm screwed. I now spend a lot of time in preparation and processing before I confront someone. That way, I can think first and then confront. Over time, I understood that fistfights are rarer than what I grew up with and that just telling someone what's up is much easier than it would appear. I now can say to someone in an unexpected confrontation, "Let me process this issue, and I will get back to you." That statement is what I need to do to be professional. I don't care what they think or what they want to do, I am going to process before I react.

I have to work hard at being myself in the real world. First, I must be okay with myself, and if I'm not, I have some shit to take to the ring.

This is practice, not perfection—another saying I got from AA. I don't believe there is "perfect." Trying to be perfect is what made me drink. Start with identifying your values, and then practice your ass off for the rest of your life. Give yourself love and grace, and realize the rest is forgiven.

Today, my responsibility to my shortcomings and failures are actually helpful to me and my businesses. Since our companies are an extension of who we are, it makes sense that our own mistakes will directly affect them. Today, I jump on those mistakes like a grenade. My point in doing so is to cover the explosion and keep the shrapnel from hitting everyone and everything around me. I immediately try to take responsibility and start looking for a solution to fix the mistake.

In this day and age, we are blown up on social media so fast that we have to handle everything fast and carefully. I am always wrong! That's the approach I take to solving a complaint, or colossal f*ck up by myself or my team. This method too, is a process of thinking before I react, but while processing, I think about how can I own this problem and make those I have disappointed come away from the situation better—especially for me or my business if at all possible. Now, of course, fixing it isn't always possible and sometimes that means an apology is the best I can do, with a promise to never do it again. Most people are happy to have someone validate them and the mistake that was made.

CHAPTER 5:

FREEDOM

> **The Worley Way**—*"I choose to live freely and with purpose. I will protect my heart and my freedom. I have freely chosen my values, and I have freely set my goals and objectives. I recognize that the failures of my past were in large part because I chose to stay trapped by my fears, guilt, and bad history. I know better now. I am free. I will freely chase my dreams. I am transformed."*

By the time I reached high school, I realized my childhood was not normal, and I needed to be free of it. I had to make my own destiny. I didn't know what I wanted or needed. I didn't have a role model or structure to guide me. I just knew I had to be free of the past. I needed to define my freedom, and it took many years to do so. To save you the 15 years of trial and error, I will break it down for you.

Freedom is different for everyone. Freedom is personal, therefore only one person can give you freedom—you. Who is in your mirror? Do you like who you see? We must love who we see or we can never meet our true potential. There are going to be times in our careers when we will face challenges, and that's when we must love ourselves, who we are, and be confident in our values. The mirror needs to represent you, not your past. The great thing about the mirror is it only shows you who you are today. It doesn't show you who you were last week or who you are tomorrow. It shows you who you are right now. It allows for a million do-overs. You can start fresh each day or each hour if you must. Nothing in your past can define today's image in the mirror. What are you doing today to make tomorrow better?

I hated the mirror when I was trapped in my vices. I saw a lost person who blew it all very young, with no chance to rectify himself. It took five years of counseling to correct that image. Bad self-image, guilt, laziness, anger, confrontation, failure, and all those things that hold you down are like handcuffs. They keep you bound from freedom and lock you away from growth. Pretty soon, years have gone by in the shackles, and you are living in sadness and talking about what "used to be."

I had to release three of my main cuffs: Addiction, bad relationships, and negative self-image. I battled addiction ever since my dad put the first pipe in my mouth. That instance was the beginning of decades of drug and alcohol abuse as well as the many reckless behaviors that accompany addiction.

My life was littered with bad relationships. Of course, that sequence started with my parents, and as time went on, it spread to the women I dated. I infected each relationship and each love with my anger, my chaos, and my addictions. I could talk a woman into believing I was a knight in shining armor, and I actually believed I was. I would seek out girls who were weak or insecure so that I could be worthy of their attention, but the relationship would eventually destruct.

Breaking the Chains

To have true freedom, we must do two things to rid ourselves of the shackles that hold us down: submit and commit.

Submit

Submitting means we admit to ourselves that we are being defined by our bad habits, emotions, and actions. We must understand and admit we have a problem in order to change it. Admit it out loud to a loved one or friend. If you can't do that, at least start with admitting it out loud to yourself. If you recognize the issue, you can move on from it. "Hi, my name is Ron, and I'm an alcoholic." I repeated that statement for weeks when I first got sober. Now, it's your turn! "Hi, my name is _____, and I have a problem with_____."

Now, that you have admitted the problem, let's get rid of it. It's time to submit to a higher power. God is my higher power, but the power of turning over to something bigger than yourself is the same. It can be anything you like. It can be a stuffed animal, if you want. God, or your higher power, is not in control of you and is not to blame for your current issues. God is the key to release you from your cuffs. When I give it to God, I no longer own it, and I can't take it back.

The method can be used for the smallest of issues, and in business or your personal life. It's highly useful when dealing with employees and with so many other issues you can't control in your business.

You have to know what is and is not within your control. There have been many times that in one business or another, we have been very slow and at times very tight on cash flow, especially in bail bonds where we depend solely on commission. In bail bonds, the risk of losing a bond to forfeiture (failure to appear in court) is high. I constantly have over 30 people and $100,000 in forfeiture. There was a time that risk would stress me out and ruin my day—every single day. I learned to just recognize that bail bonds is my job and that I am always going to have bad bonds. I now slate the time to work on the files, and I work through them for that time only. I am allowed to curse, and yell, and be pissed off during that time (sound familiar?). As soon as I am done, I get up and send it to God and let him keep it until the next time. I mentally tune out the stress from the forfeitures and go back to being productive. I do have to take it back when it's time to tackle the files again, but I don't spend the whole day stressed and worried. In my head I somehow feel that if I don't own it and I can give that stress to God, then I can be productive and earn more money to cover the bad bonds.

Commit

You have admitted, and now it's time to clean up. Commitment is the key to open the handcuffs. You have to find the right key for the particular set of handcuffs. In other words, if you have an issue with addiction, it makes no sense to go to a relationship counselor. For my addiction, I found help in AA and in a room with a psychiatrist. To let go of old recordings, I sought out a counselor. Find the right program, or the right person, or the right company. Find the right solution to follow and then commit to it.

When you are handcuffed by the police, they assume authority over you. They have the right to handcuff you based on their probable cause that you have committed an offense. You are able to release the cuffs by good behavior, time in jail, or calling a bail bondsman. When the cuffs are off, they no longer have authority. You have authority over yourself again. The same is true for freedoms. Give yourself permission to change. Decide to change. Commit to change. Once you have decided, it's time to act.

- Write it: Write down your commitment. Write down the details of the commitment—much like a New Year's resolution.
- Plan it: Plan to start this commitment very soon. Go to work on it the next day. We can't procrastinate because life

happens.
- Enact it: Make it part of your day-to-day life. Obsess on the commitment, and let it be a part of your thinking and your action each day. Soon it's just a part of you.

Be the "get shit done" person. You need to take action on your decision in order to be free. If you are in a program, then work hard at it. If you are trying to quit smoking, buy the patches, gum, and whatever else you need. If you want to be free of mortgage payments, or maybe you want a bigger house, you have to work hard for that. You might need to grab an extra job on the side to make that happen. The important piece is you must act. You are not going to lose weight by sitting on the couch. You have to get up and exercise.

Here's the thing about action: It's easy to do when you're motivated. It's difficult to do when it's monotonous. Going to the gym is easy on January 1, when you have made the New Year's resolution, but come July when you would rather go fishing, it's a lot harder to stay motivated.

It has to become part of your lifestyle. If you're trying to pay off your mortgage early, then you might need to get used to working an extra 20 hours a week. Do it over and over until you have a habit. It's okay to have habits, but we want to have good habits. See the goal and run to it! You're running toward freedom!

Freedom is an individual preference. You might not be in debt or an addict. You might not smoke, or drink, or gamble, or have any other vices. If that's you, hallelujah! Find other freedoms to sponsor. Maybe the freedom you're looking for is to travel or volunteer. Whatever it is, you need to include it in your goal sheet each year, which is a list of actionable items that you plan to achieve.

Every human should complete one, but a business owner especially needs one. The smartest time to do it is in December each year to plan out the next year with achievable goals for yourself and for your team. Make them fill one out too.

Write down four or five freedoms that you will practice this year. Put the list in a place where you will see it every day. I have mine set up as reminders on my phone. I get an alert each week with a list. I want you to articulate what you expect the result of those freedoms to be. "If I do this, I can _____." When you have this done, set them as reminders on your phone, and label them "Remove the cuffs."

We have to fight for our freedom. We must build our lives around freedom in order to achieve it. Some people in your life might not like this newfound freedom, so be prepared. They might call you selfish and self-absorbed, or even lazy.

Our freedoms are specific to us, and are in the very essence, selfish. For those of us who choose to make our freedoms part of our goals, we are going to run into opposition. When your wife or husband decides they are no longer okay with your selfishness, you must be prepared to understand a few things.

First, it's not as selfish as you might think. I learned this truth through working out at the gym every day. I found freedom in my busy work schedule to hit the gym every day for one hour. It was my hour. That hour that I spent working on just me and not thinking about work or family—or anything at all, really—was necessary for me to continue to provide for everyone. My responsibilities were easier to fulfill when I focused on me for just an hour a day.

Second, we can be too free. I was fine with the hour a day for a lot of years. Then I started doing bodybuilding shows, and an hour turned into two and then more. I would take 12 weeks to get into show shape, where I had to eat perfect, train a lot, and focus only on me the whole time. By the end of the show date, my family was sick of me. I had gone too far with this thing, and it had become unhealthy to my life as a family man.

Lastly, balance is key. We can't spend our lives free. Freedom has no meaning without work. So I have to plan bits of freedom into my life. If I go on a trip, I know my work will follow me and will be there tenfold when I get back. So I take small trips for two or three days. That compromise keeps me locked into the businesses and into my personal life but also allows me time to enjoy my freedom.

Establishing some freedoms is essential to a healthy mind and body. Your friends and family might react with jealousy if they don't have the freedoms in their lives that you will have. Fight hard and stay focused. Encourage them to find some freedoms for themselves to counteract jealousy. I promise that loved ones and friends will come around to understanding the value of freedom.

CHAPTER 6:

HARD WORK

> *The Worley Way*—*"The key ingredient to my success is my willingness to work hard. I will not be passed up by someone who is willing to work harder than I do. I will make my story one of success because I shape my life the way I choose through relentless effort and hard work. What I lack in talent and smarts, I will make up for with wisdom and hard work."*

I resolved a long time ago that no one would outwork me. Remember, I said that I run businesses to get praise from others. It's something that has stuck with me since day one of my first business of Ron's Bonds. Affirmation from others keeps me building more and more revenue and thinking of a bigger and bigger picture for my companies. Nothing is ever good enough, and everything needs more work. Of course, my resolve comes from the many years of trying to make my parents proud, and I found a way to do that through sports. I was never the best athlete, but always I worked harder than everyone on the field or mat. By working very hard, I found my way off the bench and into first string. Coaches loved me for it, which only perpetuated the need of affirmation. Before I owned businesses, I was an employee, and I desired and earned praise by way of hard work. Hard work overshadowed the fact that I was not as book smart as most.

My dad, although dysfunctional and deficient in many ways, managed to teach me the power and importance of hard work on a blistering summer day many years ago. Sweat poured down my face as I pushed the lawn mower through a jungle of grass. That chore was a typical day at work for this skinny, famished youngster. I could hear the faint bellowing of my dad's voice, "Son!" Immediately, fear swept over me, and the mower engine came to a stop as I ran across the lawn as quickly as my gangly legs could carry me. As I approached, dad motioned for me to follow him. "I need your help," he said. He wanted my help moving a large refrigerator. "Cool!" I thought. I was encouraged knowing that he thought I was strong enough to handle it.

A father's good opinion of his son is a powerful force.

If you're a father, love your kids with your deeds AND *your words. In my experience, even average dads work to show their love for their kids by bringing home a good paycheck, working around the house, fixing things for them, helping with their homework, etc., all of which is great and important. Our children need to not just see our love but also hear our love, through affirmation, encouragement, specific praise, and the words, "I love you."*

Okay, back to the refrigerator story.

"We have to get this thing out of here," he said, slowly pushing the top of the appliance in my direction. Yikes! Reflexively, I caught it in my hands—feeling the immense weight crushing my arms. Even though I was starting to panic, letting both this refrigerator and my dad down was not an option. The fear of failing my father far outweighed the pain I felt. Slowly and meticulously, we were able to inch the refrigerator out of the way. I felt elated when it was finally upright again. The look on my dad's face was worth every second of struggle. His words meant even more: "Son, you just did a man's job." I learned an important lesson that day: Hard work can do the "heart work" of building one's self-worth. This was a good day with my dad.

What is the most powerful influence in your life? Here are some ideas:

Addictions
Pride
Success
Compassion
Faith
Love

It's important to understand that these influences are your purpose. They are your driving force for hard work. If you have negative influences in your life, you will get negative results. You must rid yourself of the influences that drag you down before you can make the lessons in this book work for you. Let's think about some of these powers to take to your ring and get rid of. I have a worksheet online you can work through at www.ronworley.com.

Some common negative influences are easy to point out in others, but look at yourself while pointing them out in others. You might have issues with pride, anger, laziness, or you might surround yourself with negative people or even family members that keep you from doing the right thing. My bail bonds company is full of these influences that I have to steer clear of. I am offered sex for bonds, drugs for bonds, and the most common, stolen goods. It's to the point that the police in my local town have me investigated every few years. To them, they can't understand how I can make so much money from bail bonds. I actually put a security system in my office so that I could record the undercover cops asking me to trade drugs or other illicit things for bonds. I have stayed straight all these years, and these police that investigate just find out that I have multiple revenue streams for one, but also that I have worked so hard at our company values that damn near the entire county calls me to help them. I'm a good dude, and I run a good business.

What I'd like to help you do is figure out your "want tos" and your "have tos." I want you to tie your purpose to the "want to." So if you want to own a business and your influencer is pride, your purpose needs to be aimed at doing a good job. Your purpose for waking up every day is doing a good job for other people.

Waking up every day and going to work because you "have to" is the opposite of success. You can't maintain wealth when you live in the "have to." "Have tos" happen when we overspend, overcommit, and underprepare. Let's go through an example:

Want To:

I want a new car.
I want a new house.
I want to retire someday.
I want to pay for my kids' college.

Make a list of the "want tos" in your life now and the ones you will have some day. Both are going to be your purpose drivers for hard work. They will be the reason you wake up every day and go to work.

Have To:

I have to provide for my family.
I have to pay off debt.
I have to pay alimony.
I have to pay child support.

Whatever the "have tos" are, make the same list as you did for the want tos. "Have tos" are not always bad things. I don't want you to feel resentful or negative toward this list. I want you to prioritize the "have tos" and make them fewer than your wants. We all have them.

The trick is to always aim for the things that you want and enjoy. In the last 21 years, I always had two or more companies. What's the reason? Simple—I had one for my "want to" and one for my "have to." I needed a reason to work hard, but I also needed a little more security and steady cash flow to fund the "have tos."

Child support and college accounts were "have tos," but the nice cars and mansion on the hill were "want tos." I have always kept in mind those hot summer days with my dad while working for my "have tos." My dad showed me how *not* to live.

When I worked for my dad, I put in 50-60 hours of work a week for a whopping $50-$70 pay. There were weeks that we would work all seven days. Payday was supposed to be every Friday, but sometimes he didn't have any money left to pay me after drinking. So I kept track of what he owed me, and in my mind, I had my lists of things that I was going to buy when he finally squared up. My "want tos" were piling up in my head, but because my dad had pinned himself in a corner and had a bunch of "have tos," he couldn't pay me. Back then is when I learned about "have tos" in general. Dad never had a pot to spit in because of all the things he had to pay for just to maintain his life and his family.

My job with dad meant I was alone a lot, so I would talk to myself. I decided when I got older, I would be a better man—a man who knew the importance of working hard but also of working hard on meaningful things. I wanted to be a man who was good at both hard work and heart work.

I felt sorry for my dad, so I continued to help him. He had me brainwashed into thinking the world treated him unfairly. I mean, come on! He worked his ass off and got nowhere, right? My dad thought like many Americans in destitution. He thought if only he had a good idea, or hit the lottery, or even got a great job, he wouldn't have all his problems. The problem with such thinking is that money extenuates your personality, problems, and influences. Every time he came into extra cash, or had a good job, he would just get drunker and blow it somehow. Money came in and went out equally fast. No savings, no investments. He remained in his negative influences.

I think about my dad a lot and cherish the lessons he taught me—even when he was doing it all wrong. My dad said he wanted to be a boss, but he really wasn't willing to do the hard work or to sacrifice anything to make his dreams become a reality. He literally drank and drugged his dreams and his life away. I speak of him in the past tense because he was murdered back in 1998. He was one of multiple people murdered in my family. My uncle was murdered, my grandpa was murdered, and my father was murdered in Salina, Kansas, by the police. The news article told the story from a cop's perspective of how my dad was trying to swallow cocaine and in an effort to keep him from swallowing it, they choked him.

The truth is that my father died because he lived a certain lifestyle that only a drug dealer could afford. Not because he had nice things but because he did a lot of drugs. Dad was actually a passenger in a car on a routine stop for expired license plates. When the officers came to the car, they recognized my father and pulled him from the car. They began beating my father, and with a hard blow to the back of the head, his medulla oblongata was struck and shut down, which also shut down his breathing. They left him lying on the ground for over 20 minutes handcuffed face down, where he had suffocated. They were harassing the driver while my dad lay there, helpless.

That entire incident happened in the front yard of the EMT's building. EMTs witnessed the beating and failed to assist my father until the incident was actually called into dispatch. They threw dad on the stretcher and raced him to the hospital where he spent the last week of his life brain dead and hooked up to machines.

Never was cocaine entered into evidence, nor recovered by the doctors, nor pumped from his stomach. It was a big fat lie to cover the story of the cops on the scene. The tapes of the incident were conveniently lost, and the EMTs refused to come forward. So it ended right there. It was the one and only time that all of my father's kids were in the same room together. All six of us were in the hospital room saying goodbye.

Believe it or not, the only anger I had was that my dad and I were fighting at the time and I had not seen him in about eight months. I never got to solve my issues with him or at least talk to him about it. My dad had a chance to hold my daughter, Payton, the last time I saw him, but he couldn't because he was too high. It was the last time I saw him alive. The irony is that his girlfriend and a few of his friends all stated to me that he had been sober for two weeks when he was killed.

Dad had had his last unlucky break!

My childhood role model was dead. One would think I'd find another, but instead, his death further inspired me to be just like him. I ended up in the ditch in Nebraska, homeless, and very alone. I had worked real hard to destroy my own kids' lives, and I felt every ounce of pain that I would eventually cause them if I kept down Dad's path. As I made that long drive home from Nebraska to Colorado, I replayed my dad's life and my life over and over.

It was then that I decided my father was not going to be my role model. My stepdad would become my new father figure for advice on how to be a man and my mother for how to be sober and life advice. I was going to live the kind of life in which I would be a good role model to my kids and a mentor to many.

You might ask what makes a good or bad role model. Honestly, role models are a personal preference. I don't have role models in my life anymore; I have mentors whom I call friends. Role models tend to become flawed and human after we put them up on our pedestals by calling them "role models" in the first place. It didn't take long for my new role models to let me down. I decided to stop chasing other people's lives and to start my own. I discuss mentors in the "Friendship" chapter, where you will read that I have friends/mentors with whom I work on specific ideas. Mentors belong in the workplace for sure; role models do not. I no longer live my life to emulate someone else's. That said, I believe the parent-child relationship is the only place to be a role model. When a child becomes old enough, a good role model will explain to them that we are all flawed and will do things that they will question. That's when your child needs a great mentor.

It's All Work—Especially for Your Dreams

I respect hard work, realizing that not all hard work is the same.

Some work is hard physically.
Some work is hard emotionally.
Some work is hard intellectually.
But all hard work is worthy of respect.

We need bosses and employees. We need managers and those who are willing to be managed. We need leaders and those who are willing to follow. We need dreamers and doers. And we need those who are willing to do the hard work of making dreams come true.

As hard-working businesspeople, we must be the leader in hard work. When we lead by example, we can then influence relationships and people who work for us. Have you ever had a manager tell you to take out the trash but they never took the trash out? Let's be the opposite. We have to employ others to work as hard as we do. If you show employees through your example, they will work harder for you.

At our retail stores, we made our employees follow a closing checklist. Mostly cleaning. It was inevitable that the bathroom toilets would be neglected at some point. Shitty job—pun! I would clean the toilets myself after every shift I had to work. If I ran the store that day, I would follow the checklist to a T. I would make sure to tell the manager how awful the toilets were, and when it came time for company meetings, I would also point it out. "If I can clean, so can you."

Being a businessperson comes with permission to dream. Otherwise, what's the point? Money is only satisfying if you have dreams to make real. I am a dreamer, and I am teaching you to be a dreamer. I've learned some important lessons about dreams.

First, dreams are powerful. But unless you act on them, they will exist only in your head.

Second, some dreams can be short-lived. So work hastily.

Third, the key to making dreams come true is a commitment to doing the hard work it takes to make your dreams become a reality!

Fourth, dreams are easier said than done. Are you really willing to do the hard work required to make your dreams come true? I am, and thankfully, God sent me a woman who is as much of a dreamer and doer as I am (if not more): my lovely wife, Erin.

If you are dreaming of being rich, you need to break that down. What exactly does being rich mean to you? What house will you live in? What type of service or product will you sell to get your source of income? Make a detailed picture in your head of what "rich" looks like for you. For me, riches and dreams were not financial. My dreams contain freedom, cars, and travel. All of those require money. To have freedom and nice things, I first had to make a series of goals that would move me forward to the dream of freedom.

Building scalable companies and managing multiple businesses started with a dream to drive a nice car or to be able to fly across the country at a moment's notice. All of what our current life contains is possible because I made a choice to act on my dreams. I got off my ass and went to work. You need to act upon your dreams immediately. Go buy the house you can afford today, knowing that someday you will get the dream house. Start saving money today. Even if it's a dollar a week, start putting money away. Undertake actionable items that might not immediately give you what your dreams represent but will keep you focused and give you some confidence toward hitting your dreams in the future. Finally, work your ass off toward those actionable items. With a little wisdom on top of your hard work, you will achieve your dreams.

By the way, a bonus lesson about dreams: Dreamers who are doers attract other dreamers who are also doers. You will surround yourself with like-minded folks by simply willing yourself to act on your dreams. My wife, Erin, loves making dreams come true and is also willing to do the hard work to make dreams a reality.

One of our dreams was to own a business together. In 2010, Erin and I opened our very first Max Muscle store in Loveland, Colorado. Opening day was one of sheer excitement. Our premarketing had worked well, and we had tons of customers show up!

Let me list just two of the challenges that we had to work through in the first few weeks of opening our business...

Our regional director was pushing marketing and sales of products, and at this point, we barely knew what products we offered. We were supposed to be writing meal plans for our customers, and Erin and I had never even written a meal plan for ourselves, let alone professional meal plans for men and women who were serious athletes. Some of our customers were eating in specific ways to compete in professional body-building competitions!

I had to fire our manager for being a horrible employee, and when I sat down to fire her, I was exposed to who she really was, literally! I barely got the words "you're fired" out of my mouth before she ripped off her shirt, exposing her bra, and threw it at me. She stormed out and almost immediately began slamming us on Facebook. Part of me wanted to rip off my own shirt and quit too.

We endured. Max Muscle was making other people's lives healthier and better. Plus, it was making me, my life, and my family's life better. It mattered, so Erin and I worked hard, and great things happened.

Our first store was unbelievably successful! By the time we ended our first year in business with that store, we had quadrupled our sales and were competing to be Number One in the country. Not even a year after opening our first store, we had the opportunity to buy a struggling Max Muscle store in a nearby town, and we knew we were ready for the challenge. Within three months, we had doubled the size of the new business and brought back their lost partners. Life was good, and the work was meaningful.

I went into business to do something I love to do. But as a business owner I never got to do the things I loved. As we grew, the more time I had to put in with bookkeeping, speaking to disgruntled customers, and inventory. It was the necessary hard work toward future dreams, and with it, we got closer to those dreams. Working toward dreams involves temporary hardship, but the takeaway message is don't give up!

My wife and I were good at managing Max Muscle stores, and within a relatively short amount of time, we were managing four stores around Northern Colorado.

Erin was still working as a police officer, and I was working as a bail agent when we took over the stores. Erin was an invaluable help to me, and when she eventually retired after 12 years in law enforcement, she took our stores to a whole new level. She has a talent for building and fostering relationships in the business world and brought in many partners that we would not have had time to manage in the past. She put the Max Muscle name in our community far more than it had been in the previous years and skyrocketed the value of our company.

I like to review our accomplishments and create new ones. It's important work. I spend many nights at that bar table (my kitchen table) pounding away on the keyboard. I am completely alone, completely away from influence, and I write down ideas that come to mind. I put my raw thoughts on paper. It's a brainstorm with myself. This review/create time is important to structuring and keeping purpose in life. Try it!

I want you to find a table, or a corner booth in a bar, and answer these three questions truthfully.

1. Who am I?
2. What are my dreams?
3. What am I willing to do to make my dreams become a reality?

CHAPTER 7:

TRUSTWORTHINESS

The Worley Way—*"I will look back only to remember how far I have come. Because of the transformations in my life, I am a reliable man. The foundation of my transformation is my ability to maintain, monitor, and adjust my vocabulary and actions to be reliable. I will show up. I will work hard. I will remember."*

Just Show Up

"Dad's not coming." The words rang through my head as full disappointment sunk in. My dad wasn't coming. The anticipation that I had built up over the last few hours came crashing down as this realization hit me. He was supposed to come pick up my brother and me for the weekend. At the ripe age of seven, I simply couldn't understand why he said he was coming if he wasn't going to. I didn't know what trust was yet, but I knew that dad never seemed to do things he said he was going to do.

In my transformation from ditches to riches, I realized I could do better than my father did, just by showing up. As a father, I had to show up for everything I could, until these li'l "things" I created were all grown up. I lived and worked in Greeley, exactly 40 miles from where my kids went to school. So you can imagine the difficulty in being there for them. I was a single father of three, with my own business to run, and kids had different school activities almost every day of the week. I still made sure to show up!

Sometimes, I would drive 40 minutes to watch a two-minute dance routine or track event, and then head straight back home to finish work. I worked from 7:00 a.m. to midnight every day for 18 years, all for that moment—when one of my kids looked into the stands and could see me there. I showed up.

Brenden, my older boy, told me once, "Dad, I didn't know how hard it was for you to be there. I just knew I would look for you and you were there."

I started to use that value in business. I'd show up every day, even if for nothing else than to shoot the breeze.

It made a huge difference in our work family. One of our favorite employees, Thad, was unable to finish his school semester due to funding. We loaned him the cash to pay off the semester so that he could continue his education. We weren't asked to do it. We offered it. He was so appreciative, and it really mattered to him that we cared about his future. Sometimes, just showing up in the time of need without being asked will change an employee's life but also make them extremely loyal. It teaches them humility. It tells our team that we are there, and we have their back. In return, they have ours. It's pretty hard to steal from someone who connects to your life like that. Hard to screw over your big brother.

Showing up applies to every situation. You don't need an invitation. I wasn't invited nor did I ever give a warning. I just showed up. But I don't just show up in life. I SHOW THE HELL UP! I wear a fancy suit, $500 shoes, and a freakin' bow tie, dude! I command the room right off the bat. I want people to know I showed up. I want everyone to know I am there.

In truth, dressing up made me feel worthy to be in the room with them. This tactic boosts your self-esteem when you might not be the smartest one in the room, or maybe you're new to the industry and need to learn more before you can confidently walk into the room full of executives.

When I go to a real estate closing, I want people to ask me about my clothes and about how I'm feeling. My presentation makes my clients proud without saying words. Dress well, and treat people well. I always bring a gift for all the people in the meeting—donuts or little grab bags work well.

In our business, we want to be the one who shows up for everyone, just like we do for our kids. We are the representative of everyone who depends on us to put food on their table. We must be there at meetings, events, and community outreach. But don't just show up. You need to show the hell up!

My companies and my family work in our community a lot. We bring a team of 30 people to the food bank each month. I am on two boards for causes I care about. These are the personal things I do to help my community, but our companies are a little more selfish. We go to every 5K, every Turkey Trot, and every event that allows us to have a table. We are out there. We do the Santa Cops event, Wounded Warrior, and many more like it. We usually do an event every month. Company-wise, it shows the community that we are there for them, and we are everywhere, but personally it's good to keep up appearances and stay top of mind. I hate for this involvement to sound like we are only doing outreach for the sake of money but we currently get most of our business by way of community outreach. We draw people into our circle and raise awareness of our brands through helping others in our community.

Be sure to show up early—15 minutes early at the latest. I find myself wicked early to a lot of meetings. I use that time to settle into the situation I'm about to go into. I even throw on some Netflix in the car, while I prepare. The last thing I want to do is go into a meeting right on time or late and give off the vibe that I am chaotic and disheveled.

If you are a late person, knock it off. Stop now! It's juvenile and ridiculous. People shouldn't have to wait on you.

Put 'Em Up!

I was an emotional wreck in my twenties, and I completely blamed my parents. But c'mon—at some point I had to own this life I had made. So I did. I became accountable. My mother became the perfect example before me. When she sobered up, she had frank talks with herself and with all the people she hurt. I witnessed her own up to it all. I thought that was incredible and horrendous at the same time. And when I got sober, I knew exactly what was coming.

I used to get sick and tired of mom giving me lectures using her AA and counseling knowledge. I used to think my mom was weak because she couldn't handle her addictions. I changed my mind when I landed in the same rooms as her. I remember thinking when I first started AA that my mom quit going after a year, and I wouldn't do that. I loved AA, so why would I quit? Well, I too quit after a year, and our reasoning was much the same. We couldn't wallow in the addiction, and that's what it felt like it became after a year.

Over my recovery, I've had to practice at being trustworthy. Of course, the first part was easy. I no longer slept in late because I was hung over. I woke up early to prepare for the day. I concentrated on saying what I was going to do. If I said I would help move, then I would show up to help move. I stopped lying to people to make myself look good, which is a huge deal. Beforehand, embellishing my stories was quite common for me. I couldn't tell a story about my adventures without throwing a twist on the ending. I was a liar. I now tell the truth, show up, and be helpful to others.

I could no longer blame someone else for my problems. I had to be a problem-solver. I fought for my freedom from addiction. I fought for my beliefs in family, and I rearranged my thoughts about business. As a man of action, I had to do something in order to be something. So I positioned every encounter in my life as if I was going to fight someone. As you might imagine, that's all I knew at the time.

My business became the same. When I had a big meeting to go to, or a seminar to do, I prepared for war. I was not going to be the dumbest, least prepared guy in the room. I showed up and put 'em up. In a fight, you have to have your dukes up. You have to be ready to block and throw punches.

When you walk into a meeting, you have to be ready to hear the word "no." You might have to duck and weave and throw punches back. You must block negatives and punch with positives. This is your company, your lifeline, your baby. Fight for what's yours, and protect those in the company who trust you to put food on their tables.

Sometimes, your "put 'em up" is simply having the right slides to show or flyers to hand out. Give it all to them. You have been preparing for this fight and brought your best marketing collateral to show them. Other times, it's a conversation, and you just need to hear their needs so that you can solve their issue. Be prepared to duck and weave and throw punches.

I sit with my blue striped suit and my overpriced shoes in a room of people who expect me to be precise and to the point. I tell them what I can provide with confidence and gain their trust. If they aren't scoopin' what I'm poopin', it's their loss. I will walk with my head held high.

We give our best at all times. We provide the best products, best service, and best advice. We are helpful to others before any focus on making money, and in doing so, we are trusted. We are trusted to lead others to success.

We have very little time to make someone trust us when we meet them for the first time. In addition to changing our actions to be trustworthy, we also have to look like we are trustworthy. Companies we work for, people we sell to, and any interaction in business has very little to do with actual trust when we first meet. Nobody is going to ask if your bills are paid or if you cheat on your taxes. They are going to look at your suit and shake your hand and decide right then and there if they trust you. We need to impress them right off. But in the long run, it's your true trustworthiness that will keep them. Your actions and hard work will prove to them that they were right about choosing you.

Act Up

When we were children we were asked to behave in public. My grandma would say, "Don't act up." This admonishment was meant to stifle our behavior so that we kids didn't embarrass her. In our business behavior, I say Act Up! Go out, do what you do, and do it loud. We must show the world that we exist, show the world what we can do. Show a little cockiness about your abilities and be confident about it. Acting up is about doing whatever it is you do but doing it a little better—a little louder—than the norm.

If you are a big-rig truck driver, then drive the crap out of that truck. Innovate that truck so that you can cook and wash your clothes in it. Paint it yellow with racing stripes and run those loads. Your name should conjure up the message, "I'll get your shit there in a hurry." Act up!

What would happen if you acted up? Would you make more money in the industry? Would you spend more time at home?

Would you get noticed? Act up and find out. How do we become innovators and leaders? We act up! You become an influencer, and then people start to follow you. They trust you because you're not afraid to tear down all the walls of fear. They see you for who you are, and that is dynamic. People trust those who know who they are.

Your business image should reflect your individuality. For years, my bail bonds company never had a slogan—mostly because I tried not to bring attention to my job. Bail bonds has such a negative connotation in our society, and depending on whom I was talking to, I might not like the reaction I received. Again my reaction to their reaction could be very bad, and I never come out of situations like that looking very good. But one day I said, "Screw it!" On all the phone books and websites and online ads, I wrote, "I'll get yo' ass out" with a picture of a donkey in a jail cell. I felt I was representing myself the way I should. That sort of orneriness is exactly my character.

I'm ornery as hell. I call people on their crap, and usually I'm pretty funny. But as I ran the bail business, I kept things conservative. I worried that the lawyers and judges would frown on me for being me. It might have been me judging them when I think back on it. I imagined educated, very conservative professionals looking over their glasses and shaking their heads at my business. Maybe saying, "Ugh! This idiot is a typical bondsmen." I came to find out that most respected me as a business owner. It just took me not caring what others thought of me to change that incorrect notion.

So I tried to fit in with them instead. I ran around feeling dumb as a box of rocks because I didn't have the schooling and the experience to be in the field of law. Then I started acting up. Now, I say what's on my mind and do what I think is right, not what someone else thinks is right.

I would never disrespect courtrooms, but I also use whatever curse word that will fit the moment outside the rooms. I just keep things as real as I can and try to be authentic. There was a magic moment when I received a call to show up to the DA's office. When I got there, I was walked up the back stairs and led directly into his office. I truly thought I was in big trouble. I was sweating it big-time. The DA came into his office and shut the door and began to speak. He was asking me for a favor that only my skill set could help him with. My answer was, "Yes, of course."

That interaction started a great relationship, and our communication has been from then on awesome. Mr. DA recognized my no BS attitude, and my ability to run a clean investigation, without getting into trouble, and he rather enjoyed who I was. Today, we still are friends, even though we are the most opposite people you can imagine sitting at a table eating together. I drop my f-bombs and talk shit about our government, while he laughs and explains why my ideas won't work in politics. I'm not afraid to speak my mind anymore, nor should have I been then.

This world needs all of us. We need everyone from the overeducated, to our janitorial professionals. Look, I am not trying to run a company from my office or the bench of the courtroom, and they aren't trying to chase down bail jumpers and hustle with OGs (Original Gangsters) for a living.

I exist to help my customers. To do that, I need to speak to them in a way that they can hear me. I speak to their hearts through humility. After all, I have been to jail, and I know what they are going through. I have compassion for them, but I also know when they are hustling me and I'll call them on it. So why wouldn't I act up?

For example, I have a customer that I knew from the streets over the years. He was always good to me but very scary looking and extremely intimidating. He stood five-foot nothing and carried a large belly but also sported a bald head with devil-hour tattoos on his head and more tattoos covered his entire face. He went to jail—the first time I have ever known him to go. Usually, he is bailing out his li'l gang warriors. His wife called me to help. Charges? Sex assault on a child—$100,000 bond. I listened as the wife explained that he was innocent, but to me they are all innocent so don't judge this guy yet, my friends. I listened to her, and I trusted my gut from knowing him all these years. They had no money, and I bailed him out for free. By free, I mean free to them, because it still cost me about $3,000 to write the bond. They owed me $10,000 when he got out. But I watched as his life imploded. He lost his job because he went to jail. He then lost his home, and all the while their family was separated as he was no longer able to be around children while out on those charges. He called me every week with a new f*cked-up story about what was happening to him. A year and a half later, he beat his case in front of a jury of his peers. The whole story was made up by an ex-wife to ruin him, and it did.

Recently, I bailed out a known drug dealer, and again I used my gut to bail him out on almost $400,000 in bonds. Only this time I didn't listen to my gut: I bailed him out even though I knew better. The problem with bailing out successful drug dealers is they are no longer successful because they got caught, and they are out of income. I was owed over $30,000 when he got out. He went right back to the same ole crap, and soon enough he was doing his drugs and not paying me. I was being hustled big time. I arrested him a short three weeks after he got out and lost thousands of $$$ in doing so.

Put It Out There

I let my wife take over the social media for me under the condition that we Act Up. She started posting funny memes about jail, cops, court, and anything edgy enough to shock and awe. The sky's the limit when you're acting up. I told her to just post it, and we'd see what happened. Within weeks, we had more "likes" than ever before. Suddenly, the posts were being shared 1,800 times and were being viewed by 80,000-100,000 people each time! The attention was huge for us. People from all over America had my page. People come to my page to share on theirs. Other bail agents and lawyers have become followers. They pass around Ron's Bonds page as if I'm some channel they watch on TV or YouTube.

We need to live up to who we are, and for most of us it requires a little bravery and a "go for it" attitude—so just Act Up. In the words of Stuart Smalley, "I'm good enough, I'm smart enough, and, doggone it, people like me." Go into your community, dress up, be ready for a fight, and go beat someone's ass—figuratively, of course.

Perhaps, you're wondering how to do the three actions that pertain to trustworthiness. If I am being true to myself (Act Up), am always there (Show Up), and always fight for what's right (Put 'Em Up), do you think I am trustworthy? Can you count on me to do what I said I would do? Be trustworthy and people will trust you. I want you to get away for a bit from your "have tos" and just "be." Again, in the words of Stuart Smalley, "I'm a human being, not a human doing."

CHAPTER 8:

WISDOM

The Worley Way—*"I have lived a lot of life. I have not forgotten what I have learned through my successes and failures. Each experience has taught me something about winning. I believe I am called to offer a helping hand to those who seek it. I want to serve wisely, with confidence, and with an aura of warmth."*

In order to see how much you have grown, you must look back to where you started. It's pretty easy for me to see where I've grown in my life. I am no longer homeless, no longer hooked on alcohol or drugs, and my family surrounds me daily. I know now that I am allergic to alcohol. Every time I drink booze, I start losing my cars, my houses, my wives, and everything else in my life. That's the truth in joking—and my answer to people when they ask me if I want a drink. My life's wisdom has made me understand that I can't drink like "normal" people.

The reason I bring this up is simple. Our past gives us great wisdom in life. Had I not taken all the roads I took, I would not be successful today. Had I not failed, I would not have succeeded. Finally, had I not lived through my mistakes, I could not be living today.

Book Smart

The kind of wisdom I'm talking about here is different from being book smart (BS). I know, I know, I didn't intentionally make that acronym. However, the irony of my having the worst potty mouth in the world is not lost. BS is what we go to college for. It's the knowledge we strive for in our youth. We heard every teacher and every adult tell us to get good grades, and learn, learn, learn. We have been programmed at a young age to believe that an education leads to a good job. Sometimes, it does, and sometimes it doesn't.

I am not saying this ideology is bullshit. I am saying it's only half the truth. Education and knowledge play a huge part in your career. I have been in numerous meetings with someone who is very smart and instantly they throw out big words—words that almost flaunt their degree in your face. They are intimidating, or at least they are trying to be. I am trying hard to not offend anyone here but these guys annoy the heck out of me. Overcoming other people's bullshit took me years to master. As a person who never finished college, I took their fancy BS as an insult to my education, or the lack thereof. I struggled with whether I belonged in the meeting with them. I spent the first part of every meeting sizing myself up to the worth of their education.

If you are a book-smart person, power to you. In this day and age, we have a lot of people going after degrees. I really commend you on your ability to apply yourself to education. I have a nephew that reads all the time. He is able to educate himself on all sorts of topics, and while talking to him you suddenly realize this 12-year-old is smart as hell. He's a human Google.

Reading is his way of learning, and it works well for him. But it doesn't work well for all of us. Take a trip we all went on to Alaska last summer to fish, for example. I had to be shown how to fish in that area. Alaskans call it "flipping for reds." My nephew pulled out his pole and started fishing. Like an old pro, he started catching fish right away. When we were done on the first day, I asked him how he learned to flip. He told me that he read how to flip for reds and just tried it when we got there. That ability was amazing to me! I personally am an audio book kinda guy.

I listened to *Think and Grow Rich* by Napoleon Hill. This book was obviously written back in the early 1900s, judging by the way the author spoke about people in that time, referencing money in nickels and dimes to purchase goods. His values still are valuable today, though. The idea is to think like a rich person. Imagine yourself rich, make your goals become reality. I believe in his idea of dreaming of success and you will become successful. As a kid, I knew I would have money. It was so important to me then, and as I grew up, I made it my main focus. Money, money, money. I never knew as a child how I would be wealthy, I just knew that I would be. Later, I applied focus and purpose to a job/company that I never dreamt of being in. As a bail bondsmen, I saw huge potential in income earnings and bullied my way into making money. My mother played a huge part in my bail bonds success, but where others would be happy with making six figures a year, I looked for the next level constantly. What else could I do to make more money? How can I triple my efforts without tripling my work load? By simply knowing that I was going to make more, I found a way to make more. I did not settle for what I had. I sought out bigger and more. I overextended myself to force me to work harder, and I hit my goals as much as I could. Fall short of them? I pushed them up higher the next year. Think and grow rich.

It is absolutely pertinent to everything we want to do in business to educate ourselves in the industry. That's not all it takes, though. We have to be wise, and BS is only half of wisdom.

Street Smart

Once I became a little more self-aware, I started to realize I had something that book smart people didn't, and it was the reason I was a great bail agent. It's called street smarts (SS)! This acronym can also stand for "shit storm," which is the only thing I can think of when describing an arsenal that only consists of street smarts. SS people have characteristics of a survivor. Instincts, intuition, and honor, to name a few. I have the hustle. I can understand people and situations. I have the ability to make money from anything. No doubt my skill set came from being poor as hell as a child. This half of wisdom would be another reason I was successful.

SS is the ability to read people and leverage their emotions to get a deal done. SS is the ability to converse in a room full of strangers. SS doesn't require reading. It calls for creativity to be your biggest asset. My street smarts came from a childhood of learning to be safe in adversity and trouble. I learned how to outmaneuver the abusive people who lived in my house. In doing so, I protected myself and my brother, and even sometimes my mother. I learned through experiences and doing. True SS is a learned behavior through experiences in our life. Mostly out of fear of danger.

I can name a million times when street smarts helped me in my professional life. I have become a human lie detector and can recognize bull pucky when I hear it. I can see through people's stories, and I know when someone is being honest. I know when a person has what it takes to be successful. I use this ability to psychoanalyze a person to decide whether or not I will do business with them. If I decide to do business with them, they have to be willing to do all the legwork to get it off the ground. I can guide, but I am done working my butt off for someone else's dreams only to find out they were hustling me.

BS+SS=Wisdom

In college (the two years I attended), I invented a board game called "Big Beer Slam." I built it and played it, then manufactured it, and finally sold it. I used that game to make extra beer money every week. I had a plan—it was $5 a game, and I needed to sell two a week to support my habit. Yes, I mustered the ability to sell them, but I lacked knowledge of the law. I was setting myself up for a huge lawsuit. Now, it's obvious, but back then I wasn't thinking of those things. SS (street smarts) was my only tool, and I had the ability to take risks, negotiate, and even used psychology at times. In my haste, I left out the BS (book smarts): Filed no taxes, no bank accounts, no business registration, and no insurance. Does that sound like a wise thing to do?

Big Beer Slam:

SS: Inventing the game,

selling the game, earning beer money.

BS: I didn't use any, and I failed.

BS+SS: I should have licensed the game and researched laws. I was exposed to huge lawsuits for a very small profit.

As a business owner, I need BS+SS, or what I call wisdom—the combination of book smarts and street smarts. When I met Erin, my wife, neither of us were headed to greatness in our careers. I was running around in SS trying to be a businessman, and making good money too, but I lacked the structure I needed to be successful. Erin was stuck in a job that paid too little for her worth and was very limited on how far she could climb. Together, we became excellent business owners. Erin wrote policies, and I dreamt. To this day, we joke about how Erin is my anchor and I am her balls.

Bail bonds will provide a good example. To get my bail license, I had to use BS. I took a two-day course that would be followed by a large test. I studied on my own at home for weeks. I did this while working 50 hours a week. Look, I don't like to read nor do I read well, so the fact that I could focus long enough to study at all was nothing short of a miracle. Still, I spent every evening in those pages, taking notes and highlighting. We didn't have computers or internet to give us a course ... it was good old-fashion memory for this guy. Part of the class required a small test to determine our ability to take the large state test. I got 100 percent.

To dignify myself with judges, lawyers, and politicians, I used a ton of BS, but when it comes to trusting a customer enough to bail them out, I use SS—100 percent. If I bail someone out of jail and they miss a court date, what chance do you think they have of my bailing them out again? That's SS! Together BS+SS made wisdom and built Ron's Bonds, the largest bail company in Weld County, Colorado.

Now, we come to where I also tell you that I am not fully responsible for the success of Ron's Bonds. My mother, whose life I most closely emulate, started Alda Pauline's Bail Bonds in 1993, and in 1997, I joined her. She made her way as a woman in the bail bond industry, which is a difficult undertaking. I was her pupil for 16 years. Everything I know about running a bail bonds business came from her! My mom was a hard ass but very generous and compassionate. She was able to start her business as a woman from nothing. She used her wisdom and her experiences in her own past life to relate to her customers. Mom was extremely street smart.

So far in this chapter:

BS: Book Smart=education, structure

SS: Street Smart=situational, risk-taking, hustle, learn from mistakes

BS+SS=wisdom

Stop for a second. Try to identify your BS and SS within yourself. Use these examples to help.

BS	SS
Reading	Manipulation
Comprehension	Intuition
Study/Research	Instincts
Work Ethics	Protective
IQ Strength	Protective
Reasoning	Fear
Things Are Black & White	Honor
Less Emotional	Immature/Emotional
Data-Driven Dreamer	Sensitivity

I do not consider myself an expert in this field, nor did I research this area before I wrote this book. These are the tools I invented to handle my own situations in life and in business. That said, I came across this article that completely backs up what I am writing (https://www.learning-mind.com/book-smart/).

Take time to read the article as it is yet another example of book smart versus street smart. Probably written by someone smarter than I am.

Once you have identified those characteristics, you will be able to recognize the traits in others. I want you to be successful, and to do so, you must learn to filter with BS+SS. We also are looking for both qualities within ourselves, because BS without SS is just BS.

Likewise, wisdom is one of the values mentioned in this book that gives us confidence. As I mentioned previously, persistence, preparation (wisdom), and practice will increase confidence. If any one of those pieces is missing, you increase the risk of failure. Wisdom decreases risk. I'm not afraid of risk, but I want it to be as low as possible. I want all the facts and wisdom regarding anything I am about to do.

When I opened a real estate brokerage 10 months after I got my real estate license, everyone told me it was not a good idea—that I didn't know enough about the business to operate a brokerage. Most of all, I couldn't get my broker's license until I had two years in the business. So I did my research on what it took to open one. I knew that I didn't want to pay high fees to someone else. So for me it was all encompassing to have a brokerage. I learned the Colorado Division of Real Estate's policies on owning a brokerage. I found out what I needed to open a brokerage—the tools, software, and programs needed to do so. I then came up with a profit analysis and budget for the startup. That's an example of BS (book smarts).

> Running any business boils down to this:
> 1. Determine your values for the company.
> 2. Build systems to run the business.
> 3. Develop capital.

I had capital, systems, and values, which are easy to come by if you're already in tune with them. What I lacked was the experience to have a broker's license. I didn't have two years as an agent. So my wife and I partnered with another duo who had the experience. They became the brokers, and we ran the business. I was super-impressed with how well we were able to start from scratch in an industry we knew nothing about and be profitable within the first month. I felt we were being wise and where we lacked experience, we found someone to fill the void. In six months, I was able to operate the entire company without stepping foot in the office. This is an example of SS.

The one thing I did not see coming was the challenges of working with others. Having business partners is very complicated. The difference in values and the difference in the way we ran business was polarizing. One thing was clear very quickly into our opening of the business—we would be wise to never partner again.

My wife and I decided to end the partnership, and we sold our half to the partners. Sometimes, the best and wisest decision is to know when to fold 'em, as the song says.

Book Smart: Knowing all the ins and outs of a brokerage. Researching laws and tools.

Street Smart: Setting up an organization that can run effectively without my presence in the building. Partnering with experienced agents. Recruiting a lot of agents to do the work.

Wisdom: Pulling it all together, and then realizing we were not in the right situation, and selling our ownership.

Necessity Truly Is the Mother of Invention

Back in 2001, I opened a fence company. I had never built a fence before, nor did we have YouTube to learn. I needed a job for my cousin, Patrick, who had been living with me for the last few months. Patrick moved from Florida. I had him move in with me after my first DUI—to drive my butt around while I didn't have a license. I paid him room and board and an allowance of $100 a week. I was really just paying my enabler. Now, I could get wasted and I didn't have to drive home. After a few months, I got my license back, and Patrick was ready to work. I had a friend, Shawn, who owned a fence company in another part of Colorado, so I learned how to build a fence from him, and then I went for it. Pretty soon, we were slammed! I had to hire several people to work for us, and the money was rolling in.

Shawn and I worked well together as he was the expert in fence-building. He taught me enough to be able to bid and sell jobs. He trained employees for me, and I ran the books and sales. Together, we were able to stay out of each other's way and build a damn good business. The partnership was great because we each had definitive roles in the company, and we allowed the other to do their job without crossing roles.

Eventually, I ended up selling the company to a friend of mine who had been working for me. This business was another casualty of my addictions. Though the partnership was great with Shawn, I ended up making bad decisions because I was up to about an ounce a week of cocaine use. I was tweaked out all the time, and most of my decisions were made based on how I felt that day. My addiction was expensive too. I would take jobs to cover my addiction and then not have the money to do the job. Today, the friend I sold the company to still owns it and he is going strong. I, on the other hand, decided fencing wasn't my gig. My point here is: I learned the business, and I learned how to build a great fence. That is wisdom I will carry forever. No, I don't have the company anymore, but I still know how to build a fence. The wisdom of a great partnership will stay with me forever.

We are constantly building fences in business—a long, straight fence. Every time we add a slat to the fence, we are building wisdom (BS+SS), and if you turn and look back, you will see a long fence line as far as the eye can see. You will see how the fence isn't perfectly straight, and it changes height with the contour of the ground, creating a perfect line of imperfections. That's wisdom.

CHAPTER 9:

POSITIVITY

The Worley Way—*"I'm positive that no one likes negative people, so I choose to live a confident and positive life. I recognize that I have been my own worst enemy at times, for many reasons. I will no longer get lost in my story or in the story of others. I choose to BE positive even when my emotions or life's circumstances would suggest differently. We are not defined by our failures but by how we use our failures in a positive way."*

In 2016, I took my kids and wife to Alaska. It was the first time my kids had been to the town I grew up in. I wanted to take my boys to see where the magic happened, to see my old football field. Some people take trips to see the sunset over the Pacific Ocean in California or breathtaking views of Niagara Falls. Not me, man—I love the Wasilla High School football field in all of its glory. Surrounded by large pine trees, the field was painted perfectly with a giant warrior on the 50-yard line. I remember the noise from the fans would bounce around in the tree bowl and consume the field. It would amp us up out there, and when I visited, the feelings flooded in again. The grass field I remember sliding around in was now turf, and the stands were tiny in person compared to the stands of my memory.

We were able to go to the field and throw passes—not as a football player but as dad, husband, and business owner. My team is now my family, and they were there for me that day. I feel like I spend my life supporting others, and in that moment, I felt the support and love of my family like no other time. I scored many touchdowns on that field, and on that day I stood proud of the accomplishments from my past and my present.

My family had the opportunity to see a positive time in my life. The trip to Alaska will go down as one of our best trips as a family. It will also serve as a memory to my life for them. Hopefully, when they think of me, they will think of the Alaska trip. It's no different in business interactions. When a customer comes in, you want them to have a positive experience. The atmosphere needs to be set according to the feeling you want them to have. I always play music in the background as it takes away the awkward silence in the room. When you go into a furniture store, what does the salesperson ask you to do? Sit in the chair! They want you to feel comfortable in the furniture so you will buy it. The right atmosphere is positive reinforcement to your company, so provide the same setting in what you do. Make a list of five things you can do to change the mood in your company.

Here are some ideas:

- Music
- Lighting
- Massage chair
- Furniture arrangement
- Post your values on the wall
- Art made by employees or their families
- TVs with fun programs playing on them
- Paint the walls in the office with whiteboard paint or chalkboard paint
- Hang pictures of your employees and their families on the walls

Be Your Own Best Definition

I called my football coach to come to the field, and when he arrived, he got a great big bear hug from me. This man in my youth was a father figure and a positive person in my life. Seeing him as an adult brought back a flood of emotions—mainly gratitude. I was proud to introduce him to my family and for them to hear about my good ole days. I was thoroughly prepared to hear about the negativity but was surprised that he didn't remember any of that.

What I thought was a point when my life turned for the worse turned out to have no bearing on my legacy in his eyes. He saw a bright and athletic kid who loved the game and supported younger players. Coach knew full well that I had an issue with alcohol in high school, but he didn't think it defined me. Learning that was an awakening for me.

If others in my life don't see alcohol defining me, why should I? After this realization, I was eager to tell him where I was now in life, about the success I have had in business, and the success of my children and my wife. Coach showed me that there have been streams of positive people in my life that have created the patchwork of my past and future. I have learned to look at my past in a positive light!

In that moment with my coach, I realized that I, as a business owner, dictate the culture of the business. If I spend the whole time griping about the problems of the business, then the employees will too. As an employee, if you hear negative talk, you are going to transfer negativity to the customer. If I can squeeze the positivity out of each one of my employees, then my business will feel positive to my customers. The rumor mill, the bad attitudes, and anything else negative are not allowed in my businesses. I don't give them any power: I breed positivity. There are two big values of positivity that we must know and implement:

1. Shit rolls uphill.
2. Celebrate the wins.

I never complain to a subordinate—never! Complaints go to my wife or one of my five friends. I have taught my managers, secretaries, and employees the same thing. If my manager has an issue, and especially if it's with me, they need to tell me, not other employees. Employees are the bottom rung of the success ladder. It is the most important rung in the ladder. The bottom rung is your first contact for your clientele, and to keep the customer happy, you must have a strong bottom rung. We don't want to perpetuate the rumors or instigate disgruntled behavior. We, as owners, need to nip any negative behavior in the bud and build a positive culture in our company.

I think of my employees the same way I think about my children. I raised my kids free of the stress of my problems. Bills, schedules, and all the adult stuff is trickled in as they got age-appropriate. We want our kids to be happy and free of the responsibilities that drag down our lives. I lived a childhood caught up in my parents' drama. My mom leaned on me as her partner. When Mom didn't come home after work, it was up to me to get us home from school, do our chores, feed us, and finally get us to bed. I remember that the stress of Mom being gone kept me up all hours. I would try to sleep but would constantly wake up to see if she made it home. I lived in a pressure cooker, just waiting for the next bad thing to blow.

Saturday mornings were my respite. What was I going to do with my day of freedom? No school, and mom was off work many Saturdays. My brother and I were so happy at that moment. I would eat some cereal in front of the TV, watching all of the greatest cartoons. There was nothing like it! We could easily occupy three hours on Saturday morning while Mom slept in. I was free from getting ready for school or watching over my brother. I was without a care in the world. Those Saturday mornings are some of the best memories of my childhood at my mom's house. They were centered around positive moments of freedom.

I want my employees to feel like it's cartoon day every day! If it's cartoon day for them, they are free to be happy when a customer walks through the door. Happy employees=happy customers.

Erin was really good at creating a happy atmosphere. She would put up decorations for every holiday, and on the off months we had "summer" theme or "fall" theme decorations everywhere. We play music through the office and in the stores, and even let the employees pick their music. TVs ran videos of our events and random fun things from the community. Sure, people get used to seeing this stuff, and employees saw it as yet another obstacle in starting their day, in getting all that set up, but it set a scene for their workplace. I would rattle off the question of the day and each person had to ask that of their customer. "What's your favorite place to swim?" They would be required to ask the customer that question and write down their answer for a chance to win a T-shirt. The employee was challenged to ask that oddball question and get out of the sales box in doing so. For more information on this subject read this article: "Loosen Up! Having Fun at Work Is Good for Culture" (https://www.businessnewsdaily.com/9640-fun-at-work.html). I found it to further support my theory on creating a positive work environment. Some of the ideas I have and systems I implement have zero science, but on this one there is actual data to support what I already knew from experience. It tells us that if you have an idea, then f*ck it! Try it!

On the other hand, as much as employees can have a positive impact on the culture, one person can tear it down. Like a virus, one negative rumor will infect the entire company. If employees are negative, I fire them. If they start drama, rumors, and/or complain, I fire them ...

The second value, and the most fun, is to celebrate wins. I try to celebrate all the small and big wins, including birthdays (that's an easy one). I make sure to recognize the employee's child who won a scholarship or the playoff game. We announce wins across the company and blast them on social media. This attention helps parents celebrate and feel proud. When an employee has a personal accomplishment, I give them an attagirl (or boy). I might let them go home early one day or buy them lunch. I try to buy lunch for our employees at least once a month. Whatever I do, I try to make it cartoon day every day!

Let's bring Thadious back into the mix for a bit. Thad was a brilliant sales person. He talked to people, and people loved him. Thad was up here to go to college, and his family was miles away. We made him a part of our family and aside from the daily question-and-answer sessions I had with him, he was a sponge who just soaked up everything. We threw birthday celebrations in our stores for him, and you could see the boy glow. Thad had such a connection with us that when he decided to move on, he sought out another Max Muscle store to work for in Seattle where he would relocate. He didn't want to leave the atmosphere of our store, and it was much like sending off a child to college when he left. We let him settle in Seattle and, of course, we had daily question-and-answer sessions via phone. In about a month, we took our family (his surrogate family) to Seattle to visit him. We just popped into the store without warning. He damn near cried! I knew we touched his heart that day. It was like he relaxed in his seat for the first time in a month. Thad today is the most successful employee we have ever had. Making big money!

If done right, good things can be more contagious than bad things. You just have to bring it to light. Nobody wants to tell their friends that they work for a crappy company. They would much rather work for a great company. I try to show them why we are great.

The choice to be positive is easy at times, but we are not always happy to be at work so it takes conscious work to maintain positivity. It can be tricky because it's easy to complain and gripe to others. It's easy to forget about the mood and just work, work, work. As an owner, my job is much more than the company's production or the revenue stream. I am a teacher, a parental role model, or a big brother/sister. I am building company culture. I am responsible for my employees' careers and I'll be damned if I'll make them hate their job at my company.

Wake up today and be positive. Every day is new, and every day requires a positive wake-up. I hate ickiness in my life: Icky people get kicked out, and icky situations are worked through quickly. There is a solution to every problem and, therefore, ickiness will be subsided. Choose this outlook to be your life. It is a choice. Yes, things will happen, and you will have bad moments, but such moments do not define your life. We as leaders need to be positive in order to be successful. It has to be who you are in order to breed it into your work environment. Customers and employees do not want to be around an Eeyore personality (from *Winnie-the-Pooh*). I have never seen an Eeyore company be successful. Be Pooh instead. Let's be clear: You have to be a Pooh in order for your company to be a Pooh. I say again, and I know you know this by now: your company is an extension of you!

How can you make every day "cartoon day"—in your life and at work? Can you be a positive mentor, employee, or boss? As an owner, can you make systems or surprise the crew with a "cartoon day?" Employees can make a promise to spread the positive vibe at work. Employees can make or break the company on attitude alone. Can you be a positive leader?

CHAPTER 10:

FRIENDSHIP

The Worley Way—*"I choose to be a better friend. By living the values of this book, I will create lasting friendships. There is power in purposefully investing our time to be a great friend to our family, our staff, and our clients."*

It has been a wild ride to write this book. I first vomited on paper by telling my story to someone who would type it for me. I came up with a real piece of shit. I sat on that and even called it a book when I spoke about it. I told my friend, Arron Chambers (recognize the name?), that I had this book, and he told me about the seven that he wrote. I asked him for his help. Arron took a small flip through my book and could tell it was not a book. He had his work cut out for him if he was going to help me.

Arron took me under his wing, and with his coaching, I began to formulate an audience and a plot. Soon, I was writing my own book and with direction this time. We met weekly and read it through, diagrammed on a white board. After a few months, I had a real book—this book you are reading today. Arron had to be honest with me and tell me that my writing was not great in order for me to get better. I have now learned to be an author by jumping in and trying it. I did the "f*ck it, try it" method. By way of Chambers of fire.

Speaking of Arron, he is a pastor at one of the largest churches in Greeley. Imagine watching your pastor read this book aloud, and tell me you wouldn't switch the "fuck it, try it" method to the "F*ck It, Try it" method? Ha Ha.

Arron stepped in and helped me on a promise that I would listen and work hard, and when the time came, I would acknowledge him in this book. Make no mistake: These words are mine and mine alone, and the story sure isn't Pastor Arron's, but in no way would you be reading this book or coming to a seminar/speaking event without my good friend, Arron. Our friendship has turned into a helpful tool for others. Success.

A friend and mentor of mine told me once that business was about relationships, but who has time to be a friend? If you want to be a good businessperson, you better make time. Establishing relationships in business is the single most important aspect to being successful. It's not what you know, it's who you know. Haven't we all heard that a million times?

Relationships are grown, and they are groomed. You put work into them, feed them, water them, caress them, and whatever else you need to do to keep them healthy. Why? It's simple: When I need something or I need a favor, I go to my phone and find the person that will help me with that favor. I have friends who are senators, congressmen, authors, developers, and teachers. I have friends all over the place. In every aspect of life, I have friends. I can usually pull strings to get anything I need when I need it. I share this not because I'm bragging but because I believe it's much easier to run my businesses with the help of these relationships. Most importantly, our marketing is so much easier when our customers are our friends. I have a built-in customer base for every company I open. Here is your new motto: never burn a bridge before you have crossed it.

I believe relationships are broken down into two types: Friendlies and friends. Friendlies are those people you see at parties or in the community as you run errands. You can call upon them for little favors or use their expertise in their field. They are really awesome people to know, but you haven't spent the time to make them a friend. These acquaintances may call upon you to help them too, but you would never tell them your darkest secret.

Friends are very different. You trust your friends and they trust you. These people are like-minded, and you enjoy being around them. You can spend time with them, thus the reason you have invested time to call them friends. Usually, a friend is someone you have built history with. Friends can be hard to come by. I personally have five friends to whom I can say anything, within reason. Think of your friends as your roundtable or personal board of directors.

Your roundtable might consist of a businessperson, spiritual person (mind-body-spirit), purpose person, and your "ride or die" person. These categories can be whatever you like, and you can have as many as you want in the categories, but remember these people require you to invest time with them—we are not using them. However, be aware that these true friends will consume your time. Personally, I enjoy time with my friends, and it doesn't feel like a requirement. My best friend moved to Greeley to be closer to me, and instantly the time restraint became an issue. I now must juggle time with my best friend, my kids, and my wife. But it's worth it.

Here's an exercise that will help you figure out your relationships. Draw one circle in the middle of a piece of paper. Then draw four circles around the middle circle. In the middle circle, write "like minded" or "values." Then write the four categories of friends in the other circles. Once you figure out the categories you need, start filling in the circle by adding names. This is like being the president and choosing your cabinet. The only difference is that you like your cabinet. I'll tell you what and why I chose my categories.

"Ride or Die" Friends

I have two "ride or die" friends. These guys and I have spent lots of time together over the years. We have a lot of history. They have seen me at my worst—my very worst. Like I have, both friends have gone through stuff in their lives, which I also helped them with. We are equally in each other's debt. Each of these men share my values. They also have their own values that they developed through their own adversities.

My "ride or die" friends are the ones I can call for anything. I can brag to them and I can cry to them. They judge me—you can bet on that—but they keep it real with me. They tell me things I don't want to hear but also celebrate my successes. These are the two guys I would do anything for. I would die for them. Some would call us brothers from another mother. They're not friends by chance; they are friendships that I have raised and invested in. Most likely, you have these friends too, but you are going to start to use them and trust them like never before. It's okay, because you are going to call them and tell them they can use you too. You're giving and getting permission to be "ride or die" friends.

Business Friends

I have one of these, and he is exactly what you think. I can run anything past him that is related to business. He has a lot of book smarts, and because I am the street-smart person, I always want people in my life that fill my voids. The business friends category might have many friends in it for you, but for me they are interchangeable. I had a person who I considered my friend and all we did was talk about business—the very business we both owned in separate towns. We were tight! A few years into our friendship, he sold and moved away. I never heard from him again. So that's why I say these friends can be interchangeable. I'm currently having coffee every couple of weeks with an old friend who will fill this role for me someday. I'm investing time in that friendship now.

Spiritual Friends

My friends in this category also have changed over the years. When I was drinking and using drugs, these friends were people I smoked weed with and got super-deep with. Now, my spiritual friends are more like the people I can stay accountable to. My friend Jim is my go-to. He keeps me accountable to my values. He is also my biggest cheerleader. Jim is my man-coach-turned-friend. We hit it off on all levels as we worked together but were not real friends until I adopted my values—The Worley Way. We were then able to speak on the values level. I will call Jim when I need direction or correction or help with my purpose. He has been given permission to put me in line when I need it. Usually, the conversation is fairly equal. I'll tell him my story, and he will tell me his. Jim does not judge; he just helps me find my purpose.

Purpose is important for adults. We need a reason to get up in the morning and to stand up to adversity. My purpose is to guide, teach, and help others. My family comes first, then the community. When I get off track, I can call Jim, and he will put me back into motion. There is a purpose within the purpose. Wait, what? Here's an example: Today, I woke up and brushed my teeth. There is a reason I brush my teeth every morning—I don't want to have dragon breath all day. That said, if I don't brush my teeth, I can't do my job effectively. I will blow ass-breath all over coworkers, and I would be constantly trying to hide the tartar on my teeth with my lips when I smiled. This defect would tarnish my work, my reputation (eventually), and be super-embarrassing to me and my family. I would eventually be out of work, lose all my employees and my companies. Then I wouldn't be able to afford my bills, feed my family, or pet my dog. Right? Maybe that's a bit of an exaggeration but you see my point.

Jim speaks to me using only values. Like a preacher who would use the Bible to relate to a married couple having issues in their marriage, Jim uses values. Just like a believer of God listening to the preacher, I can only hear Jim because, I too, believe in my core values. The commonality allows us to be honest, speak without emotion, and helps me realign my purpose by using my own values. It's a "giant, spiritual, accountability friendship." Some people might choose preachers or friends from church. I also believe in those avenues, and I am spiritually connected to God, but today I am able to feel connected to God because I live close to my values.

My everyday purpose for getting up and going to work is to support my family. That's my purpose in life and my identity. That's my "have to," but it's also my value. Bottom line is if I don't brush my f*cking teeth, I can't feed my family. So you can see the purpose within my purpose.

It's a really good idea to leave emotion out of the spiritual friendship, at least while talking about values and purpose. Of course, we care for each other, but we set that aside and look at things through the lens of values. I could not disappoint the person, Jim, because it's not Jim I am talking to. I'm talking to the person who is mirroring my values back to me. This form of communication takes out the feeling of judgment, and disappointment, from the person I'm talking to and makes me accountable for my own crap. I had a few issues with my kids as they grew up—just like everyone does. Jim would say something like "speak to their hearts." It means speak to them from my values and show them how they broke those values, but also correct them with those same values. It's not personal to them when we speak with values. The kids wouldn't hear how they failed me, but rather failed the value. I say something like this to them: "I love you but we live according to these values."

Let's get your purpose on paper. Write down your five reasons for waking up every day. These can be goals too, but the purpose is more like the picture of your family or your dream nestled in the mirror of your car visor. When it's tough out there, you open your visor and look at the picture to remind yourself why you're putting up with the crap. Write down five purposes, and stick them on your visor.

Executer Friend

The executer is the friend that promotes getting things done. Do the work! This friend might be side-by-side with you. They will have a life emulated to yours. You push each other to work hard, stay within values, and generally execute your workload. This friend would most likely be someone close to you who understands your home and work life. They will hear you out when you have had a long day but also cheer you on and celebrate when you reach milestones. This friend is more like a partner and will share your same goals, whether it's in your business or theirs. Sounds like a spouse, right? It definitely can be. This friend has key components that I personally wouldn't want a wife to participate in.

- One: They drive you to do better. They create that competition within the relationship that keeps you driving forward. Who is working harder, doing more, doing better? If they land a key client or buy a new car, it makes you want to do it too.
- Two: They work just as hard and smart as you do. This similarity enables great ideas and brainstorming sessions but also keeps you focused on yourself and your performance.

I want to always be equal to them, and in order to do so, I will have to work just as hard.

- Three: They play hard. Celebrating success is so important, and your executer must be able to celebrate your wins and you theirs.

I have an executer friend with whom I partner on a few things. Currently, we are running a podcast for entrepreneurs. My executer gets stuff done and pushes me to get stuff done. I am sure that I push him back, because we often fight over who is going to do what, trying to take more work than the other. We are constantly brainstorming, and we even will just turn on the camera and talk, talk about ideas that eventually turn into revenue streams and business ideas. It's super fun to watch as one little idea can grow into a business within minutes of going back and forth. Together, we are strong, but each of us has different talents to offer the relationship.

Friendlies

Friendlies are the bread and butter of your business. They are the people you invite on social media to come to your party. You can have unlimited friendlies. They support you and your company. They are your target market.

I have been grooming my friendlies for many years. These folks are the reason I can decide to be a painter one day and instantly have an audience to sell my paintings to. They support you because they like you, not because your product is great or because you have something tangible.

Your friendlies are your street team. They are out there talking to their circles and referring their friends. Friendlies are a billboard with legs. You want to build your street team as large as possible. Groom them and do wonderful things for them, such as giveaways on social media, appreciation events, dinners, and parties. Make them special to you and their loyalty will increase.

CHAPTER 11:

FAMILY

> ***The Worley Way***—*"Before all others, family represents those who live in my home. I extend my family to those we love and know or even grew up with if they choose to respect us and our values. My family is my most valued possession. They are the mirror of my soul."*

My last name has been a pinnacle possession since birth. "Worley! We are Worleys!" my dad used to say. He said it from the top of a coffee table in his tighty-whities. Dad made us shout it back the right way. We shouted with our li'l voices, "Worley!" (pronounced war-lee). We are warlords, warriors, fighters, and we are damn proud of that. We come at you strong. Worleys don't ask for permission; we ask for forgiveness.

Your company's "family" has to be a pinnacle possession too. Employees do three things when they feel their work environment is like a family:

1. They work harder.
2. They work for less pay.
3. They stay longer.

Which result in my action as their boss:

1. Honoring their hard work.
2. Paying them more.
3. Rewarding their loyalty.

I want to offer you three of my family values that were useful to my businesses: identity, community, and vulnerability.

Identity

My mom was 16 and my dad was 18 years old when they had me. They married shortly after they found out I was on the way. My dad was a car enthusiast. He was always tinkering with the car in the garage. I remember him with grease on his hands and dirt under his nails. My mom was a thin, black-haired hippy-type. Mom was beautiful and had an attitude that challenged everyone. She would not be torn down by anyone and worked hard to prove her worth. Both of my parents were hippies, and they made us the same. To further my hippieness, I had long blonde hair, like a girl, with greenish blue eyes, and the nickname of Buster.

That was my identity until I was 30 years old. I lived up to the "Worley" name by fighting, drinking, and generally being a dick. When I sobered up, I realized that my failures up to that point in my life were because I was a "Worley." I realized that the identity my father gave me no longer worked for me. I needed my own, thus in my own family, we have the "Worley Way."

I came up with the 10 values called "The Worley Way" that I represent as chapters of this book.

- Bravery
- Confidence
- Freedom
- Hard Work
- Trustworthiness
- Wisdom

- Positivity
- Friendship
- Family
- Happiness

Now, I have something I can speak to when someone asks me who I am. "I am Ronald Lloyd Worley II—a trustworthy, family man, free from my past and positive about my future."

When Jim Hensel and I came up with "The Worley Way," it gave me the tools to teach my children how to identify with their name. We are Worleys, and you can pronounce it any damn way you want. I will live up to that name and practice every day to better myself. It was our life-blood when the kids hit their puberty years. In the same way, I gave core values to our company, Max Muscle. Instantly, the employees embraced the identity. Family, community, and health were included in everything we promoted. We hired according to those values. We were attracting bigger partners and customers with the same values. The whole company had something all could follow and grasp. We had a common identity that was tangible.

I suggest you meet with Jim Hensel at Mayhem Mindset to help you organize your values, write your own code, and understand your identity. Go to www.mayhemmindset.com to find out how Mayhem is neither the only coach out there, nor is it mandatory to pay someone. A good spiritual friend can be a fallback plan. You can also look for successful people in your area and buy them coffee for the sole purpose of getting to know them. Ask them straight up what their values are. Someone buys coffee for me at least once a week. I am always happy to talk to anyone about values and business. Once you have core values to call your own, then post them up in your company and talk about them. Bring them up every chance you get. It's the first step in building your work family.

Community

Neither my mom nor my dad really had any plans for their lives. They just worked and had kids. They divorced when I was four. My brother Leslie (Les) was the blue-eyed look-alike of my father. They were alike in every way. The chaotic life of living between two addicts was a lot for me and for Les to bear. Dad habitually beat his women, and I can't count how many times I witnessed sex, drugs, and beatings in both households.

My grandma was our savior, as she desperately tried to make our lives have some semblance of normalcy. She was our sitter most of the time, and we were employees on her farm. That's a joke, but she did work our asses off!

Grandma invented community outreach. She was constantly helping someone or volunteering somewhere. She built the first-ever firework show in Fort Lupton, Colorado. Guess who she dragged along with her? Yep, Les and me. We hated all the crap she made us do, but over time we learned the importance of giving back. Grandma had a following, and every time she planned an event, she had people there. They were people she thought of as family too.

My wife, Erin, also is all about community outreach. We spend most of our time running our business from the community perspective. We invite the community to be a part of our company.

The very definition of community requires people like all of us to get involved. Everyone and all types are welcome in our communities. That's the purpose of community in general: to put different kinds of folks in the same place to have them come together for one common good.

Testimony

Ron has been an inspiration to our Board of Directors for our nonprofit organization. We have been friends for a while, and

*I decided to ask him to join our executive board of directors.
The reason I did is because he's an outside-of-the-box thinker.
He comes up with fresh new ideas for business on how to make
things work. I am a very visionary person and have great ideas,
but he puts the details with the great ideas and makes them
come into reality. I always appreciate his advice and wisdom in
areas of business. He has added value to our executive board of
directors and continues to. You've heard the saying "anything is
possible"—he has proven that to be true.*

LAM Ministries

Community also means doing things together with people you
care about. We had monthly dinners for our employees instead of
meetings. We had events in the store where all of the employees
would come and participate, and we held competitions within the
company to further create community. Every quarter was some
sort of in-store event, usually coupled with a sale. Our favorite
was ladies' night, which we held every October. The idea was to
give ladies, especially new ladies, a chance to come into the store
without fear. The fitness industry can be very scary. Like working
out at a gym full of huge, buff dudes. Like there is any chance
to feel strong when the guy next to you is bench pressing four
times your weight. The concept of safety in women-only settings
was quite successful. Eventually, we allowed our male employees
to participate but they always had to dress up. Some years they
dressed like women, and others in sombreros, but always we
served drinks and chocolate and set up vendors from our local
community to be in the store. Not only were women able to buy
supplements for their whole family but they would get goodie
bags as well as skin-care samples and purses. We even had chair
massages set up in the back of the stores.

Other events might feature a guest speaker of celebrity status,
such as Denver Broncos players or UFC fighters or even themes

like Pee Wee football night. Anything that would bring in a specific audience or fan base that might not ordinarily come to our store or be a customer.

It's so important to us to keep our doors open to those who want to come in. Mentor people, volunteer, offer your support, and give back. All of it will strengthen your actual family and your company family.

Watch for those who think open door means unlimited access, however. Sometimes, that open-door policy got us into trouble, especially for Erin.

She was mentoring a girl at her police department who was a student at our local college and wanted to be a cop someday. Over time, Erin invited her to do things with us and our group of friends who work out together. Long story short, Erin had made her upset at some point over something barely memorable at all, and it set her off. She came to our house and was beating on the door and yelling at Erin through the front door. We had to get a restraining order on her.

Remember the movie *Single White Female*? It portrays a young women who befriends her roommate and eventually starts to dress like her, wear her hair like her, and eventually takes over her life. It's a horror flick! Erin seems to turn her male strays into one of them and makes men fall in love. Some men thought that because Erin was being kind and helpful, she wanted to sleep with them.

One time, she helped a friend of hers at work lose weight. During that time, she invited him to our family outings and to be part of her friend group. He was with us all the time. But over the course of 18 months, things turned creepy.

Erin is so pure of thought, and loyal, that she totally missed the creepy cues. One man called me and asked me to do him a favor. "Ron will you make sure Erin takes her medicine please?" Red flag number one! Eventually, she realized he was keeping tabs on her at work. He knew where she was all the time. He would pop up in the same place or call her and drop hints that he knew what she was doing. Long story short, he had been watching the GPS that was on her squad car all day. He had notes on her and even positioned his office next to the ladies' locker rooms so he could "accidentally" run into her.

The lesson here is that not everyone we are meeting in the community has good intentions. Community outreach solidifies family but invites vulnerability—the third prong to your work family.

Vulnerability

In 2011, we hired a friend of ours, Tilly, to work for one of our stores. Her personality was wonderful, and she came from a values-based family and raised one of her own. Everything about her screamed "perfect." First day of training, I could tell we had problems. Tilly was great with customer service but lacked the ability to handle stress. She really dove into the customer experience that we preached at the store. She would spend an hour helping each customer if she could, but when it came time to manage others, or deal with criticism, she froze. Tilly wanted all the good parts of the job and none of the hard stuff. We actually created a new position just to keep her in the store. She was kicking butt, all the way up to the part where we asked her to work between two stores. We knew Tilly before we hired her, but I had gotten really close to her while she worked with us. I had opened up about the woes of running the company and even asked for her counsel on family issues. We were tight. I gave her my friendship. I began to see Tilly struggle between the stores, and I had many meetings with her to try and find out what we could do to help her. Every time I talked to her, I would see fear and sadness in her eyes. She was not happy. The job had become too much for her. This is a good place for me to admit that I was not yet polished at speaking to subordinates. I probably came into each talk frustrated and gruff. After almost a year, Tilly walked off the job right in the middle of her shift. It ruined our friendship for quite a while. Today, we are buddies again and chalk this time up to inexperience on both sides. While it was happening, I went through a series of emotions: Anger, rage, shame, embarrassment, and acceptance. It was the first time I realized that I can't hire my friends and that I can't truly friend those I hire. As a boss, I had allowed myself to get too close that I failed her. I failed to recognize her strengths and her weaknesses. Worse than those two failures, I failed to motivate Tilly and coach her on her own goals.

Tilly let me down but also lifted me up, as I learned a very valuable lesson. I can treat my employees like family but I cannot befriend them and still be successful in the end. The key word in that sentence is *treat* because family is a bit of an illusion. Yes, even your real family is an illusion of sorts. That imaginary feeling of comradery—that somehow your bloodline binds you and your family together. In fact, most of the people in your family would not be in your life otherwise. Most of our bloodline offends us, bullies us, abuses us, and lies to us. Yet here we are trying to emulate family in the workplace. We are emulating the vulnerability of family and the comradery of the bloodline. That's the glue of a great team at work. We as the boss must recognize that all of our employees can be family—our children, if you will. They can feel comradery, trust, and friendship with each other, but you must remain in complete awareness that once you are vulnerable to the feeling of family, you risk failing your employees if you can't separate your responsibilities as their boss. It's smoke and mirrors that you create to make an awesome company, not a new bloodline. We have the friendship chapter to use for ourselves, and our work family is a creation of yours to feed and grow as you see fit for the absolute success of your company.

I want you to understand that I have been hurt by my employees! I have been let down and robbed too. That's okay! I have reaped the benefits of good people. We must trust our employees to truly welcome them into the family. By being open about our values, and especially our family values, we give trust to the people we are with. We hope they will absorb the values and grow with them. We must do this—it's what families do.

If I hire you, I am going to trust you until you show me I can't. When you are born into a family, it works the same way. I do a really good job interviewing new employees and can sniff out most everyone. So if you get hired, you are family. All in, no questions. If you screw that up, though, it will hurt you more than it will hurt me.

Sometimes, that means it's the *finale*, but I do allow myself to be vulnerable as I'm willing to give second chances. It depends.

When we sold our first store we took our best employees with us to work in the other stores we still owned. DJ was given the opportunity to come with us, but he turned it down. He wanted to stay in Fort Collins, where he lived. Makes sense, but it was a total slap in the face, as I had trained him myself and brought him up to be our manager. Great kid, and he went on to do great things after leaving us. He is one of the doctors who worked for us.

DJ had a meltdown and had done some wrecking of the company a day or two before the store was to switch over to the new owners. He met the new owners, and at the last minute decided he couldn't work for them. We were willing to fight for him, and he seemed truly upset that he had made a bad decision in the first place. DJ was young and confused and clearly didn't recognize the "big brother" safety net we threw over him by bringing him in the first place. Then he basically spit on our plans for him in the company, but I recognized his heart was in the right place. He just was confused and scared to make the wrong decision. I coached him and told him to trust me, that I'd take care of him. DJ was one of our most memorable employees out of hundreds. Top five because I gave him a second chance.

Other times, I will listen to a lie, knowing full well that the person is bullshitting me. I never cut off my nose to spite my face, though. I will allow them to get away with small things for a while, but I am assessing their character, and they are unlikely to last very long. Sometimes, they might even be training their replacement without knowing it.

Vulnerability is a two-way street and the most important contributor to a close-knit family. We have to be 100 percent open—not half-assed open. Allow pain, joy, and stupidity into your life, but don't let it linger. Family is truth, honesty, forgiveness, and love. Family can also be fighting, lying, and cursing. It's all part of the family!

CHAPTER 12:

HAPPINESS

> *The Worley Way*—*"Happiness is a choice. I choose to be happy before any other emotion. I am human; I get bogged down. The path back to a life with purpose is to focus on the good, the true, the meaningful, and the blessings found in each new day."*

This chapter was originally entitled blessings. I count and counted my blessings every day. Eventually, changing the title to happiness made more sense because ultimately, I was looking for happiness. I was blessed already, but not always happy. Now, I'm happy, but not always blessed. None of us really are. I have happy moments each day, and I try to stack a bunch of those moments together.

"August 16, 2016 Post on **Facebook:**

Weld County Sheriff Office—*Today, three of our Courts Unit Deputies were going about their normal duties when they responded to a much unexpected call for service. At approximately 11:00 a.m., Deputies Kinch, Yount, and Jaramillo responded to a medical emergency in the Plaza West Assembly Room where an adult male patient was suffering an apparent cardiac arrest.*

Erin has always been fearful I'd have a heart attack, knowing that the stress I endure has always been a problem. Her fears were a long-standing joke that I would drop dead one day. On August 16, 2016, I got a little dizzy while lecturing a group of probation officers at the courthouse. I sat down on a table to shake off the dizziness. I was trying to make light of the inside joke to our crowd and said, "I'm feeling a little dizzy, but this is when Erin will tell you that I'm about to drop dead of a heart attack." Immediately, I fell from the table to the ground. Erin was the only thing between me and the carpet, as she caught my head just before it hit the floor.

Before I even hit the ground, I was choking on my tongue, my eyes had rolled back in my head, and my lips were turning blue. Erin was her typical self: She commanded the situation with a calm and methodical manner. She rolled me on my back and began CPR. Within minutes, guards from the courthouse came in and brought an automated external defibrillator (AED). The AED shocked me back to life on two occasions. In true Worley fashion, I woke up fighting like a caged tiger.

I remember the light coming back as I opened my eyes, but the recordings from my past quickly ran through my head. I was struggling to figure out why the cops were holding me down. I was desperately trying to remember, "Did I take something? Did I get shot? Was I getting jumped? What the hell happened?" In fear, I fought like hell. I was told it took six men to hold me down and finally an injection from the paramedics that put me to sleep.

I woke up in the intensive care unit and had absolutely no recollection of the preceding 12 hours. I saw my wife and my daughter standing in the room. My immediate reaction was that I hurt all of these people. My wife is a very private person and does not show emotion publicly. Her eyes were swollen and puffy from crying, and I could see tear stains on my daughter's face. In my past, I woke up in the hospital because of an overdose- or an alcohol-related injury. What had I done to land here? It took a few moments for me to process what they were telling me about my condition. For the first time, my body was failing and not because of some illicit drug or alcohol problem—at least not directly. My age (47), stress, family, and job—and certainly my history of alcohol and drug use—had finally caught up with me, and I was diagnosed with a heart condition called cardiomyopathy. My heart muscles had stretched and became thinner and were only pumping 10 percent of the blood my body needed. I was told by the cardiologist that only 2 percent of people survive this type of event and that 50 percent of the survivors die within two years. To top it off, I was informed that only 25 percent of survivors live longer than five years. So my life expectancy was grim.

I had to witness countless people come in and stare at me with a sadness about them. On one hand, it was cool to see the people that came to visit. On the other hand, it was like being at my own funeral. In walked judges, cops, lawyers, and community leaders. Every visitor came as a concerned friend. I felt the love and acceptance that I had always wanted in the business world.

My boys were champs—stoic but concerned. They brought levity to the situation and kept my spirits up. They were both present every chance they got but knew I would be pissed if they missed school or practice. Payton was distraught and found it hard to leave my side to do anything, let alone work. She was there as much as she could be.

The years of effort and work I put into living my life with purpose through The Worley Way paid off that day. All of the right people in my life showed up. People came out of the woodwork to help. Even my brother Josh and sister Brandi drove six hours from Kansas to see me for a couple hours. Finally, my brother Les came from Alaska and spent four days hanging out with me once I left the hospital.

What I really came to terms with during this difficult experience is that I am not the hardened person I thought I was. I have always joked about knowing that I would die early, but when something like this happens, the joke becomes too real. I had never feared death until that point. But laying there in that hospital bed, I really wanted to live. Ever since that day, with each day I'm given, I will live out my values so that when I do meet my maker, I will go out on top. I have a saying now that I will *live like I'm dying*.

Live Like I'm Dying

Nearly dying was as dramatic as it sounds. How do I find happiness with a heart condition? When it first happened, I couldn't see past a few months down the road. The doctors gave me a 50 percent chance of living six months. With that thought in my head, I did a lot of things as if it were the last time. I took my wife to Mexico. I took my kids on vacation and went to Florida to see my mother one last time. When you're living like that, you tend to enjoy the moments more intentionally. I was grateful for the last-chance moments I was given.

This awakening is how *live like I'm dying* started. In every moment of every day, I was lucky to be alive, and I was going to take advantage of that. I started filling up my bucket list. More important than that, I stopped doing things that were a useless waste of time. If I want to buy something now, I just buy it. If I don't want to go to a function for whatever reason, then I don't. That attitude might seem reckless for most of you, but really, it's a concept for your entire life. Take money out of the picture. Live like you're dying! There's no guarantee you will live a long life, and even if you do, the consequences of living a long life will certainly catch up regardless.

If you knew you would die tomorrow, what would you do today? If tomorrow is your last day, who would you go see, or who would you call? What would you say to them? How would you treat others? Are you going to be happy or sad? I've chosen to be happy on my way out.

There are some things I had to do before I was going anywhere. I went on a farewell tour. I wanted to say goodbye, and I wanted to enjoy some last moments with some people who were very important to me. Long lost friends, brothers, mothers, and grandmothers. I went to see them all, from Alaska to Florida. I flew to eight states in two years. My wife would even fly them to Colorado and surprise me. Erin was an absolute saint during this time. She hunkered down and held down the ship so that I could travel. She also took care of the kids so they didn't miss a beat.

These moments were so profound, and the goodbyes were so meaningful. Imagine hugging your mother thinking it's probably the last time you'll see her. My brother and I cried like babies when I said goodbye. My mother said something that I'll never forget: "Ronnie (she calls me that ... ugh!), none of us ever knows if we will see each other again, and we all are dying, you're just the only one living like it."

The visit was a great time to reflect on Mom and her influence in my life. My mother is a real woman who helped trudge women's rights forward. She showed me that true fulfillment is in the hard work that we put into our purpose. Mom was a Nike commercial before Nike was a company. She just did it. I watched that. I saw her struggle in life and saw her succeed. Not only did she fix herself so she could better represent herself but she also changed the type of person she attracted in her life (my stepfather).

By living through my mother, I did have a rough go of things, and we can blame Dad for a lot of it too. When it was time to fix my shit, however, there she was. She already set the path for me. She already had a successful journey to redemption and was there to guide me along too. Mom was there when I needed to yell at her for all the fed-up crap in my childhood, and we were able to close it down and move forward.

It almost seemed natural that I would die before her. I lived a life of pure pressure and stress, wound tighter than an eight-day clock. It was a matter of time before my heart blew up. I never wanted to go through the death of my mother, and this way I could go first, and she would take that issue for me too. Now, during the time of my ultimate passing, my mom was as Solomon and strong as ever. She looked at me with sadness but spoke to me with strength. I finally had the mother I always wanted.

Another stalwart showed up. My best friend in all the world is Shawn. We have known each other since 1991. He has always lived a few hours' drive away. This separation has been the best thing for us. We probably needed distance to stay out of trouble. Shawn was there for me when I was divorced, and he was there when I had addiction issues. Shawn was there when I was homeless. Now, in the last years of my life, he has moved to Greeley. "Life is too short to be this far apart," he said. Now, we are old enough to handle ourselves. Plus our wives have hammered us into shape.

Shawn and I bought a little boat, and made it our mission to go fishing as much as we could. We've been out hundreds of times on the water trolling for walleye in Colorado, but better yet, we have gone fishing in Alaska where we caught over 500 fish in a week. Shawn got skunked in Washington on another trip, and we all got sunburnt on the first day in Florida and bitched about it the entire week there. In San Diego, I caught a 25-pound tuna and barfed all over the boat. "Live like you're dying" isn't just an expression. It's a movement, and it is contagious. It annoys the living crap out of people who can't grasp it, and it inspires those who can. Shawn and I live blocks away from each other, and now as my health seemingly is getting better, we have adopted the LLYD philosophy as our reason to drop everything and hang out! I purposefully stay "busy enough" but not so consumed with work that I can LLYD as much as possible.

I made other changes too. In business, I decided to only have hungry, like-minded people around me. I only want those around me who support my business and care about my time. I am not interested in those who use me or step over me. If you're hungry and you want to get paid, you will be on call for me. If not, there is the door. If the people who work for you are just clocking in, then get them out of there! I pay really well so that I can slightly abuse my employees' time. I'm joking, but I do expect my employees to pick up the phone on their days off. If they can't manage that, then I don't need them. Money doesn't take time off so neither can our companies. I pay my employees to be available to me, but their admiration for the job is free. I earn their respect, but I pay for their hard work. Today, the common purpose that I and all my employees have is to make my life easier. To keep me alive and to keep me LLYD. In truth, the very thing that killed me is the very thing I am asking for from employees. Hard work! They can LLYD with their own time, but in the meantime and on my time, we just "do work."

I believe that to live the LLYD lifestyle, you must work hard to achieve the freedom. You must set up your company to live that way and have set up your past finances to be prepared for this time in your life. I believe it takes great sacrifice and might even hurt some relationships to be selfish enough to pull this off. I know I sound like a dick here. I am aware, and my family has made me even more aware at times. I hate to sound so harsh or inconsiderate, but the fact is if I don't do this for myself, no one else will. I will then die with a ton of regret and a loss of experiences. If you were given three weeks to live, would you want employees who required you to watch over them and sit in the office all day holding their hand while you spend the last days of your life trapped next to them? No! You want the employee that is willing to give you three weeks to be selfish and free. LLYD is something that I preach and teach to others, and even to my employees, but if they want to practice it, they will need to do so on their time.

I hope you can see that I mean well with my LLYD selfishness. I want you to understand that this lifestyle isn't about money but rather about experiences and small moments that we otherwise would take for granted. We have to learn to absorb moments with others and live through experience. We choose this way for ourselves. We choose hundreds of times a week, and when we get to choose, we are living the LLYD lifestyle. You choose to go to work, or choose to go see family, or choose to buy that car you always wanted. We even choose to be poor or choose to be rich. This entire book has led to this point where you get to choose how you're going to live, what choices you are going to make, and what experiences will you take to your life's end.

I spend my day presented with forks in the road. Left road leads to the normal work day, normal choices of living for everyone else and what others might think is best for me. The right road takes me to a place in my mind that is free and creative. The right road only concerns me: My choices and my consequences. And guess what I always say? "F*ck It, Try It." Look for things that might excite you but you won't normally do because it's irresponsible or someone said you can't do them. Say yes once and do it. Here is how we live the LLYD life:

Make plans. Stick to them and be focused on them.

- Who would you see? Make an actual list and go see them. Email and texting does not count.

- Where will you go? What places can you get to in your time off? Go if even for a day.

- You'll need time and money. So work your ass off to find both.

CHAPTER 13:

TO RICHES

The Worley Way—*"My riches are the moments I make with the people I love, and the values I instill in the lives of the ignorant."*

When I sat in that bed at the hospital, it was like witnessing my own funeral. I got to see what my mark was on other people. I not only saw who came to see me, but I saw in their eyes how they felt about me. It was profound. I took it to heart—no pun intended. Okay, maybe a little pun intended!

When I wasn't in immediate danger of dying, I decided to build my legacy. I don't mean an empire, although I have a small one of those too. What I mean is: what is your impression upon your community, your loved ones, and even your adversaries?

My idea of legacy is to be unforgettable. I don't need or want my name on a library. I am leaving my character behind. I want all the people I have ever connected with to have something fun and positive to say when my name is dropped. Honestly, I want to be so missed that people talk about me for years after my death. My kids will keep my values and tell them to their kids. My friends will tell my crazy stories with love, and strangers will miss my kindness. I won't leave heirlooms or trinkets, and the money will be spent long before my legacy dies. I only hope that in the end, I did a good job for all who know me.

Leave a legacy that doesn't only involve money. Work in your community and give when you can—not just when you want to. The high road is high—that's why they call it that. It's hard to reach, and it's a long, brutal road. You won't always want to take it, and you will have pain at times, but stay on it. It always works to your advantage. Get out there and help others. Don't give money to the guy on the street corner. Give him something that will change his life. Go out there, and do the work!

May my legacy be your story, and may you find your riches.

Acknowledgements

Thank you to the team of people who contributed time, resources, and talent to make this book a reality.

Arron Chambers
Ariel Flores
Jim Hensel
Arturo Hernandez
BJ Hill
Tyler Renken
Diane Schott
Kara White
Bethany and Jeff Wiley

Brenden Worley

Special Acknowledgement

Arron Chambers was instrumental in the success of this book. I met Arron through high school track, when my son, Brenden, ran for him. I quickly saw how well Arron communicated to his athletes. He had a way of talking to them that motivated and inspired them all at once. I then ran into him at a speaking engagement where he blew my mind with his ability to take over the room and make everyone listen to what he has to say. In my mind he was the perfect person to show me how to write a book. Arron is brilliant! He is an author of seven books himself. The combination of his writing and coaching skills really motivated me to keep writing and keep working to the end. Please find him online and see what I mean. https://www.arronchambers.com/

Made in the USA
Middletown, DE
18 October 2020